FRESH BEATS

A STANDARDS-BASED HIP-HOP CURRICULUM

ROBERT VAGI

Denise's DJ Font courtesy of Denise Busch: http://www.budeni.com

Alfred Music
16320 Roscoe Blvd., Suite 100
P.O. Box 10003
Van Nuys, CA 91410-0003

alfred.com

TABLE OF CONTENTS

CD Track Listing

1. Background #1
2. Background #2
3. Background #3
4. Background #4
5. Background #5
6. Background #6
7. Drum Set Lesson 1 – Rhythm 1 with counting
8. Drum Set Lesson 1 – Rhythm 1
9. Drum Set Lesson 1 – Rhythm 2 with counting
10. Drum Set Lesson 1 – Rhythm 2
11. Drum Set Lesson 1 – Rhythm 3 with counting
12. Drum Set Lesson 1 – Rhythm 3
13. Drum Set Lesson 1 – Rhythms 1 & 2 with counting
14. Drum Set Lesson 1 – Rhythms 1 & 2
15. Drum Set Lesson 1 – Rhythms 2 & 3 with counting
16. Drum Set Lesson 1 – Rhythms 2 & 3
17. Drum Set Lesson 1 – Rhythms 1 & 3 with counting
18. Drum Set Lesson 1 – Rhythms 1 & 3
19. Drum Set Lesson 1 – Rhythms 1, 2, & 3 with counting
20. Drum Set Lesson 1 – Rhythms 1, 2, & 3
21. Drum Set Lesson 2 – Rhythm 1 with counting
22. Drum Set Lesson 2 – Rhythm 1
23. Drum Set Lesson 2 – Rhythm 2 with counting
24. Drum Set Lesson 2 – Rhythm 2
25. Drum Set Lesson 2 – Rhythm 3 with counting
26. Drum Set Lesson 2 – Rhythm 3
27. Drum Set Lesson 2 – Rhythms 1 & 2 with counting
28. Drum Set Lesson 2 – Rhythms 1 & 2
29. Drum Set Lesson 2 – Rhythms 2 & 3 with counting
30. Drum Set Lesson 2 – Rhythms 2 & 3
31. Drum Set Lesson 2 – Rhythms 1 & 3 with counting
32. Drum Set Lesson 2 – Rhythms 1 & 3
33. Drum Set Lesson 2 – Rhythms 1, 2, & 3 with counting
34. Drum Set Lesson 2 – Rhythms 1, 2, & 3

About Fresh Beats

For as long as music education has been present in public schools, students have been able to participate in bands, choirs, orchestras, and have even received instruction in piano, guitar, and a variety of other "traditional" offerings. While these courses continue to have a strong presence, there are still many students who may not elect to participate but who are interested in and even passionate about music. In recent years teachers have been challenged to find innovative ways to involve more students in their music programs by providing a relevant and high-quality music education. *Fresh Beats: A Standards-Based Hip-Hop Curriculum* is designed to do just that. *Fresh Beats* is a resource for teachers with secondary general music classes. It includes information and resources to acquaint teachers with hip-hop music and culture, and easy-to-use lessons that teach the national standards. Students in a *Fresh Beats* classroom will learn about the history of hip-hop, critically reflect on its role in society, listen to and critique popular music, write their own rap songs, and learn to compose and perform drum beats. For teachers wishing to provide their students with a relevant, high-quality music education, *Fresh Beats* is an essential resource.

ALIGNMENT WITH NATIONAL STANDARDS

Each lesson contains a series of behavioral/learning objectives. Every objective is aligned with at least one national standard. Following each objective there is an indication of [National] Standard(s) followed by a series of numbers. These numbers indicate the national standards for each objective. The standards are as follows:

1. Singing, alone and with others, a varied repertoire of music.
2. Performing on instruments, alone and with others, a varied repertoire of music.
3. Improvising melodies, variations, and accompaniments.
4. Composing and arranging music within specified guidelines.
5. Reading and notating music.
6. Listening to, analyzing, and describing music.
7. Evaluating music and music performances.
8. Understanding relationships between music, the other arts, and disciplines outside the arts.
9. Understanding music in relation to history and culture.

From *National Standards for Arts Education*. Copyright © 1994 by National Association for Music Education (NAfME). Used by permission. The complete National Arts Standards and additional materials relating to the Standards are available from NAfME: The National Association for Music Education, 1806 Robert Fulton Drive, Reston, VA 20191; www.nafme.org.

HOW TO USE FRESH BEATS

Lessons are grouped by topic: history/culture, songwriting, and drum set, and will take roughly five to six weeks to complete if students meet every day. These lessons do not need to be taught sequentially, nor must a teacher use all of them.

Easy-to-use assessment tools are provided as a part of the reproducible worksheets. This makes grading easy for teachers and expectations clear to students.

Several lessons require that teachers purchase additional media. These consist of individual songs and television episodes that are inexpensive and easily found on the internet.

Every effort has been made to use musical examples that are appropriate for children. Songs that are relevant to instruction but contain sections with questionable content have been marked as "optional." Teachers are encouraged to preview all songs to ensure that they are congruent with the values of their school community.

This book comes with a *Fresh Beats* CD. The CD contains backgrounds for songwriting and recorded examples for drum set lessons.

Drum set lessons are taught in such a way that no drum set is needed. Though teachers may have individual students use a drum set, the lessons provided teach students using body mapping. This allows multiple students to practice at once without the cacophony of misplaced notes.

It is important to remember that the lessons in *Fresh Beats* are designed for use with the general school population. As such, they are often very structured. The methods suggested by *Fresh Beats*, however, are not in any way a final pedagogical authority. This is particularly true for the songwriting portion. MCs use a variety of methods when writing and not all lyrics fit the structure provided in these lessons. As a result, there may be some students who will wish to use a different method when writing. This should be encouraged.

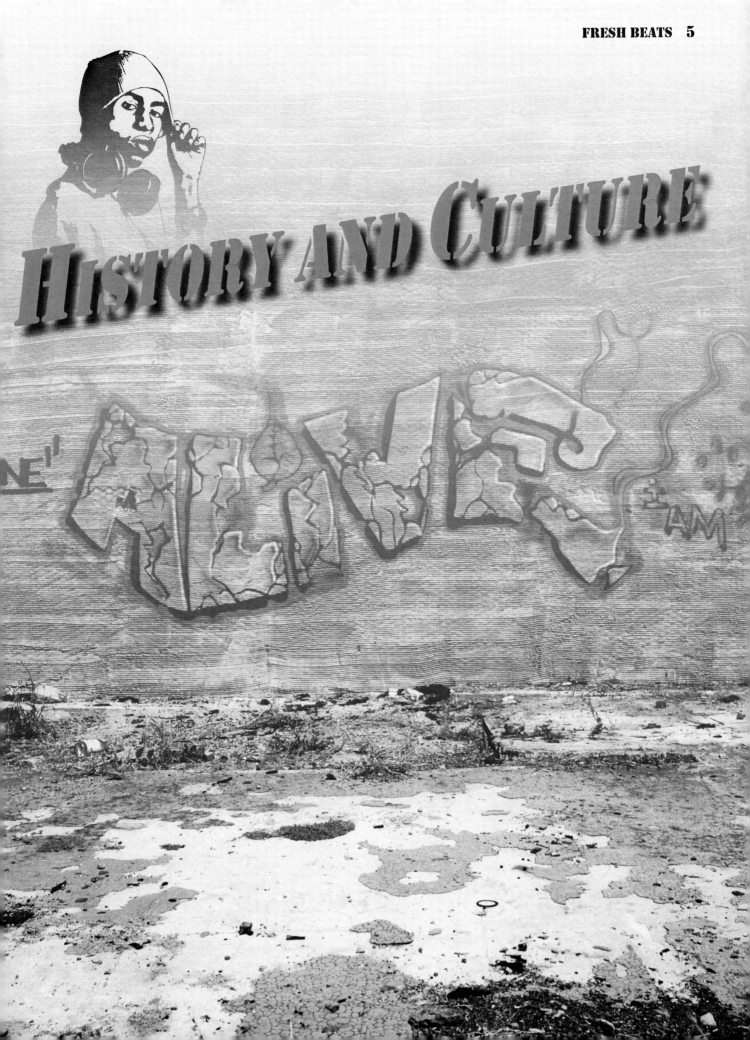

HISTORY AND CULTURE

HIP-HOP BEGINNINGS

During the 1970s, poverty, gang violence, and drug abuse were pervasive in the Bronx area of New York City. Drug dealers targeted young people and gangs made the streets unsafe. It was out of this world that hip-hop was born, both as a reflection of it and a reaction against it.

Clive Campbell, known locally as "Kool Herc" for his Herculean athleticism, was born in 1955 in Kingston, Jamaica. His family moved to New York when he was still a child and eventually took up residence at 1520 Sedgwick Avenue in the Bronx. During the summer of 1973, Herc and his sister threw a dance party using the recreation center of their apartment complex. Herc ran the music or "DJed" the party. His set list consisted largely of rock and funk music by artists like James Brown, The Incredible Bongo Band, and Jimmy Castor. The party was hugely successful and became the first of many to be thrown by DJs and MCs throughout the Bronx. It was out of this dance party movement that hip-hop was born. Because of this, Kool Herc is widely acknowledged as "the Father of Hip-Hop."

While DJing, Herc noticed that dancers got particularly excited during a song's instrumental break. In order to elongate these sections he would allow one record to play through the "break" while having another turntable with the same record cued to the beginning of it. When the first record had reached the end of the instrumental break, Herc began playing the second while preparing the first to repeat the same section. By switching between turntables Herc was able to create "breaks" that lasted for several minutes. During the "breaks," people began to dance competitively. These "b-boys" (break-boys) and "b-girls" (break-girls) became the pioneers of "break dancing."

In addition to a DJ, parties often had an "MC." Short for "master of ceremonies," MCs introduced the DJ and riled up the crowd with phrases like "throw your hands in the air and wave them like you just don't care" or "everybody scream!" Over time, MCs began incorporating elaborate rhymes and poetry. Some even formed "crews" and developed routines where multiple MCs passed off lyrics. These rhymed chants continued to evolve in both complexity and length and became what is now known as "rapping."

Before hip-hop entered mainstream culture, it was largely a local phenomenon limited to the Bronx and surrounding areas. During the early years of hip-hop there were several DJs and MCs who became local and eventually national celebrities. Two of the most prominent were Afrika Bambaataa and Grandmaster Flash.

Afrika Bambaataa was born in 1957 and raised in the Bronx. As a youth he led the Black Spades, a large and violent gang. The positive influence of the Bronx dance party movement had a profound effect on Bambaataa. Inspired by DJs like Kool Herc, he began DJing parties of his own. As a DJ, Bambaataa gained a large following and after leaving the Black Spades formed the Zulu Nation, a group dedicated to promoting peace and unity through hip-hop.

Joseph Saddler, commonly known as "Grandmaster Flash," was born in 1958 in Barbados and eventually moved to the Bronx. The most widely known DJ of the early years of hip-hop, Flash is credited with developing DJing to a level of artistry by refining and mastering the technique of "scratching." Early DJs realized that by spinning vinyl records with their hands and "scratching" the turntable's needle against the record they could manipulate the resulting sounds. This practice allowed DJs to transform their turntables from record players into musical instruments. Grandmaster Flash is also known for his successful recording career. As both a solo artist and as a member of Grandmaster Flash and the Furious Five he has released nine albums. In 2007 Grandmaster Flash and the Furious Five were the first hip-hop artists to be inducted into the Rock n' Roll Hall of Fame.

HIP-HOP—EMERGENCE AND EVOLUTION

By the end of the 1970s, hip-hop had spread beyond the Bronx and continued to grow in popularity. Sylvia Robinson, a former singer and record executive, realized the potential for hip-hop to be a viable genre in the recording industry. In the summer of 1979 she met Henry "Big Bank Hank" Jackson, a local bouncer and manager of the Mighty Force Emcees. Robinson approached Jackson about starting a hip-hop act. Though he was not an established MC, he agreed. Two others, Guy "Master Gee" O'Brien and Michael "Wonder Mike" Wright, joined Jackson and formed the Sugarhill Gang. In late 1979, with the help of Sylvia Robinson's newly created Sugarhill Records, the Sugarhill Gang released "Rapper's Delight." "Rapper's Delight" was the first hip-hop recording to be released to the public. While its release is widely considered to have been the birth of mainstream hip-hop, "Rapper's Delight" was controversial among early DJs and MCs. There were several reasons for this. The members of the Sugarhill Gang were not widely respected or even known as MCs among the hip-hop community. Also, Grandmaster Caz of The Cold Crush Brothers originally wrote Henry Jackson's lyrical contribution to Rapper's Delight. Jackson, who once managed The Cold Crush Brothers, "borrowed" the lyrics but never gave payment to Caz. Finally, Rapper's Delight used the backgrounds to Chic's "Good Times," a popular disco song at the time. Disco, however, was rapidly losing popularity

among young people. Those familiar with hip-hop felt that this further distanced "Rapper's Delight" from the music and culture that they helped to create. Though "Rapper's Delight" was not without controversy, it opened the door for other MCs and DJs to enter the music industry.

Kurt Walker, commonly known as Kurtis Blow, was born in 1959 in Harlem, NY. He took part in the early hip-hop scene as a b-boy and DJ. In 1976 he enrolled in the City College of New York and served as the program director for their radio station. In 1979 Blow recorded the single "Christmas Rappin,'" a hip-hop take on "The Night Before Christmas." "Christmas Rappin'" was released through Mercury Records, making Blow the first hip-hop artist to sign with a major record label. In 1980 Kurtis Blow released his second single "The Breaks." "The Breaks" was a huge success and sold over 500,000 copies, becoming the first rap song to be certified gold.

In 1983 a group by the name of RUN-DMC gave hip-hop its first overhaul. Raised in the Hollis neighborhood of Queens, New York, the members of RUN-DMC represented a new kind of hip-hop. Their aggressive look created by black jackets, black pants, laceless Adidas, brimmed hats, and gold chains stood out from the sleek and sometimes eccentric look of other artists. RUN-DMC also brought a new sound to hip-hop. The invention of the drum machine allowed them to depart from the funk backgrounds that

had been prevalent up to that point. With edgy, aggressive lyrics and sparse, heavy-hitting backgrounds RUN-DMC changed hip-hop forever with their 1983 hit single "It's Like That/Sucker MCs." Several groups followed suit and became very successful including The Beastie Boys and LL Cool J.

HIP-HOP: 1980s

The 1980s saw a surge in hip-hop's popularity. Hip-hop's increased popularity gave many "authentic" MCs a chance to share their music with the world. Also, as hip-hop spread across the country, artists with a variety of cultural backgrounds and messages emerged. A growing demand for hip-hop artists allowed record labels to recruit and shape new artists. Though the rise of pop rap created many one-hit-wonders, there were many pop rap artists who had very successful careers and created a large body of work like MC Hammer and The Fresh Prince (Will Smith). Pop rap, by definition, was intended to be "popular." Its goal was to reach the broadest possible audience. For many "original" MCs, this often came across as being superficial or "selling out." Artists "from the streets" often had to tone down both their image and their message while other artists attempted to appear more street-wise than they really were. This trend angered many loyal hip-hop artists and fans.

Despite the rise of pop rap during the 1980s, there were still many artists writing about serious issues. Public Enemy often spoke as the voice of a disenfranchised urban community. Their music was aggressive and politically charged, frequently challenging the status quo and bringing to light issues that were otherwise ignored. Known for his lyrical prowess, "Rakim," (born William Michael Griffith) also wrote socially conscious music. Topics ranged from leaving a criminal life-style in "Paid in Full" to a critical look at war in "Casualties of War." There were also a number of female hip-hop artists who used their music as a platform for discussing issues specific to women. Queen Latifah (born Dana Elaine Owens) began her career in 1989 with the release of "All Hail the Queen." Several tracks from this album like "Evil That Men Do" and "Ladies First" deal with the empowerment of women and women's rights. Salt-n-Pepa, an all female hip-hop trio, also used their music to deal with women's issues with songs like "Ain't Nuthin' But a She Thing."

THE 1990S AND THE RISE OF GANG RAP

Though gang rap had been present since the mid-1980s, it was not until the early 1990s that it took center stage. Claiming to document authentic experiences such as living in urban poverty, gang rap (or gangsta rap as it is commonly called) is known for its graphic and often controversial subject matter. Because of its content and rapidly increasing popularity, gang rap became a topic of concern for parents and politicians alike. Fears arose regarding hip-hop's influence on young people. If they listened to music glorifying destructive and often illegal behaviors, would it encourage them to do the same? The debates surrounding this issue lead to the creation of "explicit lyrics" labels that are now found on recordings with questionable or suggestive content.

During the mid-1990s gang rap was given significant media attention because of an increasingly tense feud between East Coast and West Coast rappers. This is often referred to as the East Coast/West Coast Rivalry. The controversy centered largely around rappers from two record labels: Sean "Puff Daddy" Combs'

New York-based Bad Boy Records and Suge Knight's California-based Death Row Records. The two most prominent figures in the dispute were Tupac "2Pac" Shakur and Christopher "The Notorious B.I.G." Wallace.

Shakur, whose parents were actively involved in the Black Panther movement, was born in 1971 in New York but later moved to Marin City, California. As a youth he studied the arts extensively including theater, dance, and poetry. At the age of nineteen he joined California-based rap group Digital Underground as a roadie and dancer. After making several appearances with Digital Underground he released his first solo album, "2Pacalypse Now." Shakur signed with Death Row Records in 1995 when, after serving eleven months of a prison sentence, Death Row's CEO, Suge Knight, posted his $1.4 million bail.

Wallace was born in 1972 in the Bronx. He became involved in crime at a young age and by the time that he was twenty years old had been arrested multiple times. Rapping had been a part of his life since he was a teenager

and after being featured in Source Magazine's "Unsigned Hype" column, he was signed to Uptown Records in 1992. He quickly left, however, to sign with newly formed Bad Boy Records. Wallace became close friends with Bad Boy founder and CEO Sean Combs.

Though tensions between East Coast and West Coast rappers had existed prior, the feud between Shakur and Wallace began in 1994 when Shakur was shot multiple times in the lobby of a Manhattan recording studio. He later blamed Combs and Wallace for setting him up. Rappers from both coasts quickly took sides. What followed was a flood of albums filled with taunts and insults directed towards the opposing group. Though violent outbursts between factions were common, when an unidentified gunman murdered Shakur in 1996 the entire country took notice. Wallace was murdered a year later in a similar fashion. They were twenty-five and twenty-four years old, respectively.

After their deaths, a truce was called followed by a decline in the presence of gang rap.

2000S AND BEYOND

The 2000s saw the rise of the rapper/entrepreneur. Artists, encouraged by financial success and aware of their celebrity status, expanded the scope of their careers. Artists like Queen Latifah and Will Smith made names for themselves in Hollywood, starring in films like "Hairspray" and "Men in Black." Sean Combs (now known simply as "Diddy") and LL Cool J have started their own clothing lines. Artists like Flava Flav of Public Enemy and Joseph Simmons (Run) of RUN-DMC have appeared in their own reality television series.

The 2000s have also seen a rise in criticism by those who claim to represent "true" hip-hop. They feel that much of today's rap music glorifies materialism and promotes misogyny and that there is an overall lack of creativity and depth. Artists like KRS-One and Mos Def are leading this movement by calling artists to write music with meaningful messages and to use their music as agents of change.

What started as a modest dance party in the Bronx has turned into a worldwide phenomenon. Mos-Def once said, "I love hip-hop because it forces people to rethink what a group of disenfranchised youth from the ghetto are capable of." Often maligned by adults and embraced by youth, hip-hop has always had the power to give voice to those who otherwise would have none. This ability to empower is what gives hip-hop its universal appeal. When hip-hop was first introduced to the public it was dismissed as a fad. Nearly thirty years later it is one of the most popular musical genres in the world. There is no telling what the future holds, but one thing is certain: as long as there are people with something to say, hip-hop will endure.

FOR FURTHER READING

Can't Stop Won't Stop: A History of the Hip-Hop Generation by Jeff Chang

The Hip Hop Wars: What We Talk About When We Talk About Hip Hop—and Why It Matters by Tricia Rose

Black Noise: Rap Music and Black Culture in Contemporary America by Tricia Rose

Hip Hop Matters: Politics, Pop Culture, and the Struggle for the Soul of a Movement by S. Craig Watkins

Book of Rhymes: The Poetics of Hip Hop by Adam Bradley

How to Rap: The Art and Science of the Hip-Hop MC by Paul Edwards

Rap Music and Hip Hop Culture by Richard Mook

The Vibe, History of Hip Hop edited by Alan Light

LESSON

BEGINNINGS OF HIP-HOP

Objectives:

- Students will describe how rapping and break dancing started. – Standard(s) 8, 9

- Students will describe the influences of Kool Herc, Grandmaster Flash, and Afrika Bamabaataa on the history of hip-hop. – Standard(s) 8, 9

- Students will evaluate an early hip-hop song. – Standard(s) 7

- Students will describe why they either liked or disliked an early hip-hop song. – Standard(s) 6, 7

- Students will identify instrumental breaks. – Standard(s) 6

- Students will compare and contrast early and contemporary hip-hop from the point of view of an early DJ. – Standard(s) 8, 9

Lesson Length: Approx. 90 min. (2 Class Periods)

Materials:

Recordings of:

- "I Got You (I Feel Good)" by James Brown
- "Freedom" by Grandmaster Flash and the Furious Five

Pencils

Student Worksheets/Artist Summaries

Procedures:

1. Give students five minutes to write down everything that they know about hip-hop using the "Hip-Hop – Beginnings Writing Prompt" worksheet.
2. Have students share their answers with a partner.
3. Ask for volunteers to share their lists with the class.
4. Read the following to students:

   "Very few styles of music can trace their origin back to a single date. However, many people believe that 1973 was the beginning of hip-hop. Today you are going to learn about how hip-hop started. You will also learn about some of the people who helped create it."

5. Divide students into three groups. Assign each group to read and complete a summary for one of the following artists: Kool Herc, Grandmaster Flash, and Afrika Bambaataa.
6. Ask each group to share their summary with the class. Provide corrections and clarification as needed.

7. Read the following to students:

    "Most of us have listened to hip-hop music before. One thing that usually sets it apart from other kinds of music is rapping. Rapping is when words are spoken rhythmically with music. This is different than singing because singing requires the use of musical pitches. Rapping, like break dancing, came out of the dance parties that took place in the Bronx during the 1970s. DJs often invited friends to "MC" their parties. Short for "Master of Ceremonies," MCs introduced the DJ and riled up the crowd with phrases like "throw your hands in the air and wave 'em like you just don't care," or "everybody scream!" Over time, MCs began incorporating elaborate rhymes and poetry. Some even formed "crews" and developed routines where multiple MCs passed off lyrics. These rhymed chants got longer and more complex and eventually became what we now know as "rapping." Most early MCs rapped about themselves or about having fun. Their messages were usually positive. Early hip-hop was an alternative to the gangs, drugs, and violence that were prevalent in the Bronx at the time.

8. Have students form groups of three. Each group should have one representative from each of the previous groups.

9. Have students work collaboratively in their groups to complete the "Hip-Hop Beginnings" worksheet.

10. When students have completed the worksheet, read the following:

    "You read earlier that hip-hop started with a series of dance parties. At these parties, DJs usually played funk and rock music which often had instrumental breaks. An instrumental break is a section of a song that uses only instruments. Kool Herc used two turntables to make the breaks longer. People began dancing competitively during the longer instrumental breaks. These competitive dancers became the first break-dancers. I am going to play "I Got You (I Feel Good)" by James Brown, a famous funk and soul artist. When you hear the instrumental break, raise your hand."

11. Play "I Got You (I Feel Good)" by James Brown. Students should raise their hands at 42" and 1'22"

12. Read the following:

    "You read earlier about Grandmaster Flash. He was one of the few early DJs to have a successful recording career. His album The Message was the first hip-hop recording to deal with issues facing urban youth. Please take out the Hip-Hop Beginnings evaluation sheet. I'm going to play a song called "Freedom" by Grandmaster Flash and the Furious Five. Please fill out the evaluation page while the song plays."

13. Play "Freedom" by Grandmaster Flash and the Furious Five. Point out the "breaks" at 1'20", 2'30.

14. Ask students to share their responses to with a partner and then with the class.

Assessment:
"Hip-Hop Beginnings" worksheet
Music evaluation worksheet

HIP-HOP BEGINNINGS WRITING PROMPT

Write down everything that you know about the history of hip-hop in the space below.

_____

_____

_____

_____

_____

_____

_____

_____

_____

_____

_____

_____

_____

_____

_____

_____

artist profile

DJ Kool Herc spins records in the Hunts Point section of the Bronx at an event addressing "The West Indian Roots of Hip-Hop," February 28, 2009.

Clive Campbell, known by his friends as "Kool Herc" for his Hercules-like athletic skills, was born in 1955 in Kingston, Jamaica. His family moved to New York when he was still a child and eventually settled in the Bronx. During the summer of 1973, Herc and his sister threw a dance party using the recreation center of their apartment complex. Herc deejayed the party, playing mostly rock and funk music by artists like James Brown, *The Incredible Bongo Band*, and Jimmy Castor. The party was hugely successful and became the first of many to be thrown by DJs (disc jockeys) and MCs (master of ceremonies) throughout the Bronx. It was out of this dance party movement that hip-hop was born. Because of this, Kool Herc is widely considered "the Father of Hip-Hop." Kool Herc, unfortunately, never recorded an album. He did, however, make an appearance in the 1988 film "Beat Street."

While deejaying, Herc noticed that dancers got particularly excited during a song's instrumental break. In order to elongate these sections, he would allow one record to play through the "break" while having another turntable with the same record cued to the beginning of it. When the first record had reached the end of the instrumental break, Herc began playing the second while preparing the first to repeat the same section. By switching between turntables Herc was able to create "breaks" that lasted for several minutes. During the "breaks" people began to dance competitively. These "b-boys" (break-boys) and "b-girls" (break-girls) became the pioneers of "break dancing.

artist profile

Joseph Saddler, commonly known as "Grandmaster Flash," was born in 1958 in Barbados. His family eventually moved to the Bronx area of New York City. He was one of the most famous DJs from the early years of hip-hop and is best known for developing "scratching." Early DJs realized that by spinning vinyl records with their hands and "scratching" the turntable's needle against the record, they could make several different sounds. This allowed DJs to turn their turntables into musical instruments. Grandmaster Flash is also known for his successful recording career. As both a solo artist and as a member of *Grandmaster Flash and the Furious Five*, he has recorded nine albums. His album *The Message* was the first hip-hop recording to express the frustration of urban youth living in poverty. In 2007, *Grandmaster Flash and the Furious Five* were the first hip-hop artists to be inducted into the Rock n' Roll Hall of Fame.

artist profile

Kevin Donovan, commonly known as Afrika Bambaataa, was born in 1957 and raised in the Bronx area of New York City. As a youth, he led the Black Spades, a large and violent gang. Hip-hop had a profound effect on Bambaataa. Inspired by DJs like Kool Herc, he began deejaying parties of his own. As a DJ, Bambaataa gained a large following and, after leaving the Black Spades, formed the Zulu Nation, a group dedicated to promoting peace and unity through hip-hop. After forming the Zulu Nation, Bambaataa has worked hard to spread hip-hop to countries outside of the U.S. Though he has not received the same commercial success as Grandmaster Flash, Afrika Bambaataa has recorded over twenty albums including *Planet Rock: The Album* and *Dark Matter Moving at the Speed of Light.*

ARTIST SUMMARY

Artist/Group Name:

_____

Date and Place of Birth _or_ Where and When This Group Was Formed:

_____

Famous Recordings:

_____

Reasons They Are Important to the history of Hip-Hop:

_____

_____

_____

_____

Interesting Facts:

_____

_____

_____

_____

Hip-Hop Beginnings Worksheet

In at least *five* sentences, describe how hip-hop started and how break dancing and rapping developed. (5 points)

_____

_____

_____

_____

_____

Why is Kool Herc called the "father of hip-hop?" (1 point)

_____

In at least *two* sentences describe how Kool Herc extended the "breaks" of songs. (2 points)

_____

_____

Name one thing that Grandmaster Flash is famous for. (1 point)

_____

Who formed the Zulu Nation? (1 point)

_____

Hip-Hop Beginnings Worksheet (continued)

Imagine that you are a hip-hop DJ during the 1970s. You find a time machine and are transported to today. How is the music that you hear different than the music during the 1970s? Would you be happy with how hip-hop has changed? Why or why not? What would you tell the other DJs when you return to the 1970s? (4 points)

_____

_____

_____

_____

_____

_____

_____

_____

_____

_____

Rubric:

4 points	3 points	2 points	1 point	0 points
The response adequately answers all of the questions	The response adequately answers 3 of the questions	The response adequately answers 2 of the questions	The response adequately answers 1 of the questions	The response does not adequately answer any of the questions

Grading: 14–13 points = A, 12 points = B, 11–10 points = C, 9 points = D, 8–9 points = F

HIP-HOP BEGINNINGS EVALUATION

Use the table below to rate how well you like the song being played. Give each aspect of the music a score from 1–5 with 5 indicating that you liked it a lot and 1 indicating that you did not like it all. (1 point for each category completed)

Name of Song and Artist:

_____

Speed (Tempo)	
Changes in Volume (Dynamics)	
Lyrics/Message	
Sounds that are Used (Timbre/Instrumentation)	
Flow (Vocal Rhythms)	
Instrumental Rhythms/Beat	
Other:	
Total	

In your own words, describe what you think this song is about, who the intended audience is, and why using at least *three* sentences. (3 points)

_____

_____

_____

_____

Grading: 9 = A, 8 = B, 7 = C, 6 = D, 5-0 = F

HIP-HOP BEGINNINGS WORKSHEET

In at least *five* sentences, describe how hip-hop started and how break dancing and rapping developed. (5 points)

In 1973 Kool Herc threw a dance party in the Bronx. It was so popular that other DJs

started throwing their own parties. At these parties people would dance competitively

during instrumental breaks. This kind of competitive dancing became known as break

dancing. There were also MCs at many of the dance parties who introduced the DJ and

riled up the crowd. MCs began including elaborate rhymes. This became rapping.

Why is Kool Herc called the "father of hip-hop?" (1 point)

He began the dance party movement that created hip-hop.

In at least *two* sentences describe how Kool Herc extended the "breaks" in songs. (2 points)

He would play an instrumental break from one record while a second was cued to the

beginning of the break. When the first record reached the end, he would start the second.

Name one thing that Grandmaster Flash is famous for. (1 point)

Scratching, the first hip-hop inductee to the Rock n' Roll Hall of Fame, etc.

Who formed the Zulu Nation? (1 point)

Afrika Bambaataa

Grading: 10–9 = A, 8 = B, 7 = C, 6 = D, 5–0 = F

ANSWER KEY
HIP-HOP BEGINNINGS WORKSHEET (CONTINUED)

Imagine that you are a hip-hop DJ during the 1970s. You find a time machine and are transported to today. How is the music that you hear different than the music during the 1970s? Would you be happy with how hip-hop has changed? Why or why not? What would you tell the other DJs when you return to the 1970s? (4 points)

The music today uses beats that sound like they are made by computers. The music from

the 1970s used more live instruments. The songs from the 1970s also had positive

messages. I am happy with some of the changes that have happened and unhappy with

others. I like the sounds used in today's hip-hop. I do not like that so many songs talk

badly about women. I would tell the other DJs to be sure that we tell up and coming DJs

to keep their messages positive and to continue innovating their sounds.

Rubric:

4 points	3 points	2 points	1 point	0 points
The response adequately answers all of the questions	The response adequately answers 3 of the questions	The response adequately answers 2 of the questions	The response adequately answers 1 of the questions	The response does not adequately answer any of the questions

Grading: 14–13 points = A, 12 points = B, 11–10 points = C, 9 points = D, 8–9 points = F

LESSON

HIP-HOP — BREAKTHROUGH AND EVOLUTION

Objectives:

- Students will identify the contributions of the Sugarhill Gang, Kurtis Blow, and RUN-DMC to the history of hip-hop – Standard(s) 8, 9

- Students will respond to "Rapper's Delight" from the point of view of an early MC – Standard(s) 8, 9

- Students will evaluate, compare, and contrast two early hip-hop songs – Standard(s) 6, 7, 9

Lesson Length: Approx. 90 min. (two class periods)

Materials:

Recordings of the following:

- "Rapper's Delight" by the Sugarhill Gang (optional)

- "The Breaks" by Kurtis Blow

- "Hard Times" by RUN-DMC

Pencils
Student Worksheets/Artist Summaries

Procedures:

1. Ask students to take five minutes to respond to the following using the "Hip-Hop – Breakthrough and Evolution" worksheet: "Have you ever felt like someone was pretending to be something that they were not? Describe that time and how it made you feel."

2. Ask students to share their answers with a partner and then with the class.

3. Read the following to students:

   "Today we are going to learn how hip-hop went from something done by young people in the Bronx to being part of the mainstream record industry. The first hip-hop song released to the public made many original MCs and DJs upset. There were several reasons for this, one of them being that the people who recorded it were not known for being MCs. Many people felt that they were pretending to be something that they were not."

4. Divide students into three groups. Assign each group to read and complete summaries for one of the following artists: Sugarhill Gang, Kurtis Blow, and RUN-DMC

5. Ask each group to share their summary with the class. Provide corrections and clarification as needed.
   * *You may choose to play "Rapper's Delight" for students and explain to them that it was the first hip-hop recording ever released to the public. **However, the third verse contains lyrics that may not be appropriate for school.***

6. Have students form groups of three. Each group should have one representative from each of the previous groups.

7. Have students work collaboratively in their groups to complete the "Hip-Hop – Breakthrough and Evolution" worksheet.

8. Read the following to students:
   "Take out the 'Hip-Hop - Breakthrough and Evolution Evaluation' worksheets. I am going to play "The Breaks" by Kurtis Blow. This is one of his most famous songs."

9. Play "The Breaks" by Kurtis Blow and have students fill out the "Hip-Hop – Breakthrough and Evolution Evaluation" worksheet.

10. Have students share their answers with a partner and then the class.

11. Read the following to students:
    "I am now going to play "Hard Times" by RUN-DMC This is from their first album. Notice the use of a beat machine in the backgrounds."

12. Play "Hard Times" by RUN-DMC and have students fill out the "Hip-Hop – Breakthrough and Evolution Evaluation" worksheet.

13. Have students share their answers with a partner and then the class.

14. Read the following to students:
    "Now turn to the 'Hip-Hop – Breakthrough and Evolution Compare and Contrast' worksheet. I'm going to play "The Breaks" and "Hard Times" again. Remember that Kurtis Blow represented the "original" hip-hop sound and that RUN-DMC used their backgrounds and their lyrics to change the sound of hip-hop. Please fill in the Venn diagram comparing and contrasting the two songs."

15. Have students share their Venn diagrams with each other and then with the class.

16. Create a class Venn diagram using the students' answers.

Assessment:

Hip-Hop – Breakthrough and Evolution Worksheet

Evaluation Sheets

Venn diagrams

artist profile

SUGARHILL GANG

By the end of the 1970s, hip-hop had spread to areas outside of the Bronx as it became more and more popular. Sylvia Robinson, a former singer and record executive, realized the potential for hip-hop to make money in the recording industry. In the summer of 1979, she met Henry "Big Bank Hank" Jackson, a local bouncer and manager of the *Mighty Force Emcees*. Robinson approached Jackson about starting a hip-hop act. Even though he had little experience as an MC, he agreed. Two others, Guy "Master Gee" O'Brien and Michael "Wonder Mike" Wright, joined Jackson and formed the *Sugarhill Gang*. In late 1979,

the *Sugarhill Gang* released "Rapper's Delight" under Sylvia Robinson's new record label, Sugarhill Records. "Rapper's Delight" was the first hip-hop recording to be released to the public.

"Rapper's Delight" was controversial among early DJs and MCs. There were several reasons for this. The members of the *Sugarhill Gang* were not widely respected or even known as MCs within the hip-hop community. Also, the fact that the *Sugarhill Gang* was from Englewood, New Jersey and not New York angered many original MCs and DJs. Further, Grandmaster Caz of *The Cold Crush Brothers* originally

wrote Henry Jackson's lyrics to "Rapper's Delight." Jackson, who once managed *The Cold Crush Brothers*, "borrowed" the lyrics but never gave credit or payment to Caz. Finally, "Rapper's Delight" used the backgrounds to Chic's "Good Times," a popular disco song at the time. Disco, however, was losing popularity among young people. Many criticized the choice to use a disco background for "Rapper's Delight" because most early DJs did not play disco. Though "Rapper's Delight" was not without critics, it opened the door for other MCs and DJs to enter the music industry.

artist profile

KURTIS BLOW

Kurt Walker, commonly known as Kurtis Blow, was born in 1959 in Harlem, NY. He took part in the early hip-hop scene as a b-boy and DJ. In 1976, he enrolled in the City College of New York and served as the program director for their radio station. In 1979, Blow recorded the single "Christmas Rappin'" a hip-hop take on "The Night Before Christmas." "Christmas Rappin'" was released through Mercury Records, making Blow the first hip-hop artist to sign with a major record label. In 1980, Kurtis Blow released his second single "The Breaks." "The Breaks" was a huge success and sold over 500,000 copies, becoming the first rap song to be certified gold. Kurtis Blow became the first "star" of hip-hop. Over his eleven-year career, he released ten albums. He is known for his eloquent rhymes and positive message. After his music career, he began work as a minister by founding The Hip-Hop Church.

artist profile

RUN-DMC

In 1983, a group by the name of RUN-DMC introduced the first significant musical changes to hip-hop. Raised in the Hollis neighborhood of Queens, New York, RUN-DMC consisted of Joseph "Run" Simmons, Darryl "D.M.C." McDaniels, and Jason "Jam-Master Jay" Mizell. RUN-DMC represented a new kind of hip-hop. Their aggressive look created by black jackets, black pants, laceless Adidas, brimmed hats, and gold chains stood out from the sleek and sometimes eccentric look of other artists. also brought a new sound to hip-hop. The invention of the drum machine allowed them to depart from the funk backgrounds that had been prevalent up to that point. With edgy, aggressive lyrics and sparse, heavy-hitting backgrounds, in 1983 RUN-DMC changed hip-hop forever with their single, "It's Like That/ Sucker MCs."

Between 1984 and 2001, they released seven albums. During this time they became immensely popular. During the late 1990s and early 2000s, tensions within the group had begun pushing them apart. Tragedy hit in 2002 when Jam-Master Jay was shot and killed in his recording studio. Jam-Master Jay's death shook the hip-hop community. Joseph Simmons and Darryl McDaniels announced that RUN-DMC was officially disbanded shortly after. Both Simmons and McDaniels have gone on to record solo albums. Simmons has also starred in his own MTV reality show "Run's House."

Artist Summary

Artist/Group Name:

_____

Date and Place of Birth _or_ Where and When This Group Was Formed:

_____

_____

Famous Recordings:

_____

Reasons They Are Important to the history of Hip-Hop:

_____

_____

_____

Interesting Facts:

_____

_____

_____

_____

HIP-HOP — BREAKTHROUGH AND EVOLUTION WORKSHEET

Using at least *three* sentences, describe why original MCs and DJs were upset by "Rapper's Delight."
(3 points)

_____

_____

_____

_____

What is the name of the group who recorded the first hip-hop song ever released to the public? (1 point)

_____

Why is Kurtis Blow important to the history of hip-hop? (1 point)

_____

What is the name of Kurtis Blow's first album? (1 point)

_____

Using at least *three* sentences, describe how RUN-DMC's music and image were different from earlier hip-hop artists. (3 points)

_____

_____

_____

Put the following events in order by writing the numbers 1, 2, and 3 to the left. (3 points)

_____ Kurtis Blow releases "Christmas Rappin'" and is signed by Mercury Records

_____ *The Sugarhill Gang* is formed

_____ RUN-DMC records "It's Like That/Sucker MCs"

HIP-HOP — BREAKTHROUGH AND EVOLUTION WORKSHEET (CONTINUED)

Imagine that you are an MC in 1979. You and your friends turn on the radio and hear "Rapper's Delight" for the first time. You have not heard of the *Sugarhill Gang* and their music sounds different from the hip-hop that you and your friends have helped create. What is your first reaction? How do you feel? Do you think that what the *Sugarhill Gang* did is a good thing? Why or why not? (4 points)

_____

_____

_____

_____

_____

_____

_____

_____

Rubric:

4 points	3 points	2 points	1 point	0 points
The response adequately answers all of the questions	The response adequately answers 3 of the questions	The response adequately answers 2 of the questions	The response adequately answers 1 of the questions	The response does not adequately answer any of the questions

Grading: 16-15 points = A, 14-13 points = B, 12 points = C, 11-10 points = D, 9-0 points = F

HIP-HOP — BREAKTHROUGH AND EVOLUTION EVALUATION

Use the table below to rate how well you like the song being played. Give each aspect of the music a score from 1–5 with 5 indicating that you liked it a lot and 1 indicating that you did not like it all. (1 point for each category completed)

Name of Song and Artist:

_____

Speed (Tempo)	
Changes in Volume (Dynamics)	
Lyrics/Message	
Sounds that are Used (Timbre/Instrumentation)	
Flow (Vocal Rhythms)	
Instrumental Rhythms/Beat	
Other:	
Total	

In your own words, describe what you think this song is about, who the intended audience is, and why, using at least _three_ sentences. (3 points)

_____

_____

_____

_____

_____

Grading: 9 = A, 8 = B, 7 = C, 6 = D, 5-0 = F

COMPARE AND CONTRAST

HIP-HOP — BREAKTHROUGH AND EVOLUTION

Use the Venn diagram below to compare and contrast the songs played in class. Your Venn diagram must have a total of *ten* similarities and differences. Use the categories from your evaluation sheet (lyrics, speed, volume, sounds used, etc.) as a starting point. Only accurate descriptions will be counted. (10 points)

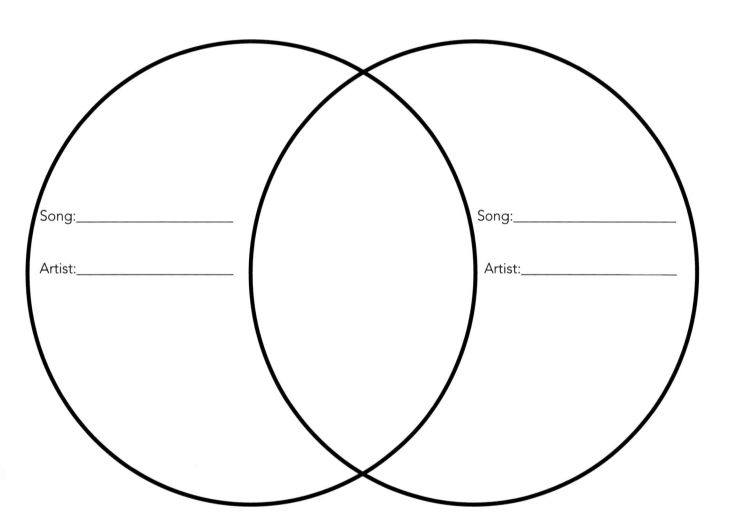

Grading: 10–9 points = A, 8 points = B, 7 points = C, 6 points = D, 5–0 points = F

HIP-HOP —BREAKTHROUGH AND EVOLUTION WORKSHEET

Using at least *three* sentences, describe why original MCs and DJs were upset by "Rapper's Delight."
(3 points)

The Sugarhill Gang were not known as MCs. Also, they were not from the Bronx. Henry

"Big Bank Hank" Johnson used lyrics written by Grandmaster Caz.

What is the name of the group who recorded the first hip-hop song ever released to the public? (1 point)

The Sugarhill Gang

Why is Kurtis Blow important to the history of hip-hop? (1 point)

He was the first star of hip-hop. or *He was the first MC to sign with a major record label.*

What is the name of Kurtis Blow's first album? (1 point)

The Breaks

Using at least *three* sentences, describe how RUN-DMC's music and image were different from earlier hip-hop artists. (3 points)

They used an electronic beat machine. Their lyrics were edgy and aggressive. They

wore all black, with laceless Adidas and brimmed hats.

Put the following events in order by writing the numbers 1, 2, and 3 to the left. (3 points)

__2__ Kurtis Blow releases "Christmas Rappin'" and is signed by Mercury Records

__1__ The Sugarhill Gang is formed

__3__ RUN-DMC records "It's Like That/Sucker MCs"

ANSWER KEY

HIP-HOP — BREAKTHROUGH AND EVOLUTION (CONTINUED)

Imagine that you are an MC in 1979. You and your friends turn on the radio and hear "Rapper's Delight" for the first time. You have not heard of the Sugarhill Gang and their music sounds different from the hip-hop that you and your friends have helped create. What is your first reaction? How do you feel? Do you think that what the Sugarhill Gang did is a good thing? Why or why not? (4 points)

I am shocked to hear hip-hop on the radio. Also, I am surprised that I have never heard

of the Sugarhill Gang. I feel excited that my favorite music has made it on the radio but

my music is better. I think that what they did is good because "Rapper's

Delight" will allow other MCs to share their music with the world. I am not happy

that they used Grandmaster Caz's lyrics without giving him credit.

Rubric:

4 points	3 points	2 points	1 point	0 points
The response adequately answers all of the questions	The response adequately answers 3 of the questions	The response adequately answers 2 of the questions	The response adequately answers 1 of the questions	The response does not adequately answer any of the questions

Grading: 16-15 points = A, 14-13 points = B, 12 points = C, 11-10 points = D, 9-0 points = F

COMPARE AND CONTRAST SAMPLE ANSWERS

HIP-HOP — BREAKTHROUGH AND EVOLUTION

Use the Venn diagram below to compare and contrast the songs played in class. Each song must have a total of *ten* similarities and differences. Use the categories from your evaluation sheet (lyrics, speed, volume, sounds used, etc.) as a starting point. Only accurate descriptions will be counted. (10 points)

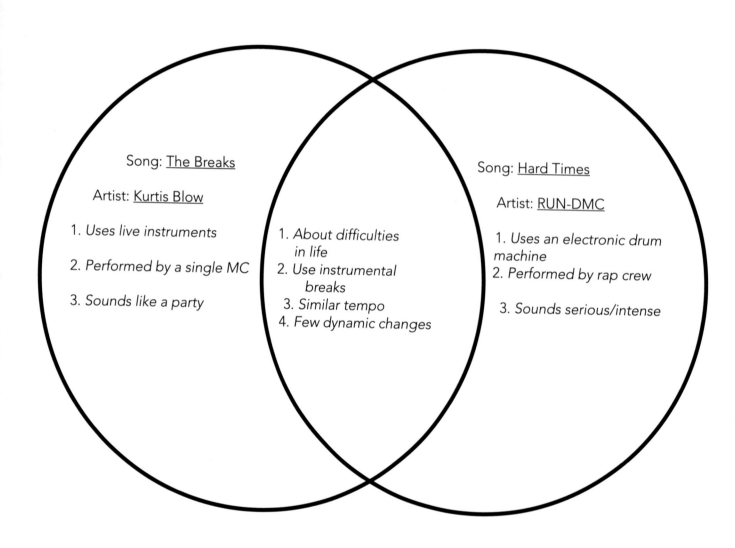

Song: The Breaks

Artist: Kurtis Blow

1. *Uses live instruments*

2. *Performed by a single MC*

3. *Sounds like a party*

1. *About difficulties in life*
2. *Use instrumental breaks*
3. *Similar tempo*
4. *Few dynamic changes*

Song: Hard Times

Artist: RUN-DMC

1. *Uses an electronic drum machine*
2. *Performed by rap crew*

3. *Sounds serious/intense*

Grading: 10-9 = A, 8 = B, 7 = C, 6 = D, 5-0 = F

Lesson
Hip-Hop during the 1980s — The Rise of Pop Rap

Objectives:

- Students will describe pop rap's significance to the history of hip-hop – Standard(s) 9

- Students will describe Will Smith and MC Hammer's lives and their contributions to the history of hip-hop. – Standard(s) 9

- Students will draw connections between pop rap and their own lives. – Standard(s) 8

- Students will evaluate, compare, and contrast two pop rap songs. – Standard(s) 6, 7

Lesson Length: Approx. 90 min. (two class periods)

Materials:

Recordings of the following:

- "Fresh Prince of Bel-Air Theme" by Fresh Prince

- "U Can't Touch This" by MC Hammer

Whiteboard/Marker

Pencils

Student Worksheets/Artist Summaries

Procedures:

1. Have students take out the "Hip-Hop During the 1980s – The Rise of Pop Rap" writing prompt. Give students five minutes to respond to the following: "What is your favorite song? Why? When you listen to a song, what is more important: the musical sounds or the lyrics? Why?"

2. Have students share their answers with a partner and then with the class.

3. Read the following to students:

   "During the 1980s, hip-hop's popularity grew quickly. Many rappers began making television and film appearances. Several artists and record labels tried to increase their fan-base by writing music that would appeal to a large number of people. This kind of music became known as "pop rap." Popular music, by definition, is meant to be popular. In order for rappers to write music that appealed to the largest number of people possible, they had to write about topics that lots of people could relate to. Many early MCs felt that pop rappers were "selling out" or not being true to the spirit of hip-hop so that they could make money."

4. Using the "Song Topics" worksheet, have students work in groups to brainstorm song topics that they feel appeal to many people and song topics that appeal to few people. Have students share their answers with the class and create a class list.

5. Based on the class list, have students decide whether or not the song they listed in their writing prompt is "popular" or not and why. Ask students to share their answers with a partner and then with the class.

6. Divide students into groups and have them read and complete summaries in their workbooks for either Fresh Prince or MC Hammer.

7. Have students share their summaries with the class and clarify as needed.

8. Divide students into pairs and have them complete a "Hip-Hop During the 1980s – The Rise of Pop Rap" worksheet.

9. Read the following to students:

   "You read earlier about Fresh Prince and MC Hammer, two famous pop rappers. Today we're going to listen to some of their music. The first song that I am going to play for you is "The Fresh Prince of Bel-Air Theme Song." Some of you may have heard it before on the television show The Fresh Prince of Bel-Air. That version was made shorter to fit the time given for the opening credits. The version that I am going to play was used in the first episode and gives a more complete background to the show. This kind of fun, light-hearted lyrical content was typical of The Fresh Prince and DJ Jazzy Jeff."

10. Play "The Fresh Prince of Bel-Air Theme Song" and have students fill out the "Hip-Hop in the 1980s – The Rise of Pop Rap Evaluation" worksheet.

11. Ask students to share their answers with a partner and then the class.

12. Read the following to students:

    "The next song that I'm going to play for you is "U Can't Touch This" by MC Hammer. It was the most popular song from his best-selling album, Please Hammer Don't Hurt 'Em."

13. Play "U Can't Touch This" by MC Hammer and have students fill out a "Hip-Hop in the 1980s – The Rise of Pop Rap Evaluation" worksheet.

14. Ask students to share their answers with a partner and then with the class.

15. Read the following to students:

    "Turn to the "Hip-Hop in the 1980s – The Rise of Pop Rap Venn diagram" worksheet. I'm going to play both songs again. Please fill out the Venn diagram, comparing and contrasting the two."

16. Have students share their answers with each other and then the class.

Assessment:

Hip-Hop during the1980s – The Rise of Pop Rap Worksheet

Evaluation Sheets

Venn Diagrams

WRITING PROMPT

HIP-HOP DURING THE 1980S — THE RISE OF POP RAP

In the space provided below, answer the following: What is your favorite song? Why? When you listen to a song, what is more important: the musical sounds or the lyrics? Why?

_____

_____

_____

_____

_____

_____

_____

_____

_____

_____

_____

_____

SONG TOPICS

Use the space below to brainstorm song topics that appeal to many people and song topics that appeal to few people. In other words, what are some song topics that many people can relate to? What song topics could only a few people relate to?

Topics that Appeal to Many

_____

_____

_____

_____

_____

Topics that Appeal to Few

_____

_____

_____

_____

_____

_____

artist profile

THE FRESH PRINCE

Willard Smith Jr., more commonly known "Will Smith" or "the Fresh Prince," was born in 1968 and raised in West Philadelphia.His mother worked for the School Board of Philadelphia and his father worked as a refrigeration engineer. Smith got involved with MCing while growing up and in 1985 met Jeff "Jazzy Jeff" Townes, a local DJ. The two formed the group *DJ Jazzy Jeff and the Fresh Prince*. In 1986, they released their first single "Girls Ain't Nothing but Trouble." The song became a hit and led to the release of their first album, *Rock the House*, in 1986, which was also very successful.

DJ Jazzy Jeff and the Fresh Prince continued to record and in 1988, they released the album *He's the DJ, I'm the Rapper*. *He's the DJ, I'm the Rapper*'s hit single "Parents Just Don't Understand" went on to win the first ever rap Grammy. By the time the group broke up in 1993, they had recorded five albums. The group became known for their clean and fun lyrics.

By 1990, hip-hop had become so popular that it attracted the attention of the television network NBC. They approached Smith about starring in a television sitcom about a street-smart teenager who leaves West Philadelphia and moves in with his rich aunt and uncle in their Bel-Air mansion. The show was called *The Fresh Prince of Bel-Air* and ran for seven years. This was a significant step forward for hip-hop. By using a rapper as the star of *The Fresh Prince of Bel-Air*, NBC acknowledged that hip-hop's popularity had grown to a new level.

Smith went on to have a successful career in film. He has starred in blockbusters like *Men In Black*, *Independence Day*, and *Ali*. He has also released three solo albums since he and Jazzy Jeff separated.

artist profile

MC HAMMER

Stanley Burrell, better know as "MC Hammer," was born in 1962 and raised in Oakland, California. As a child, he would often sell stray baseballs and dance for money outside of the Oakland Coliseum. One day the owner of the Oakland A's saw Burrell and was impressed with his energy. He offered him a job as a clubhouse assistant and batboy for the team. While working for the A's, Reggie Jackson started calling Burrell "Hammer" because of his resemblance to Hank Aaron.

Burrell went on to join the Navy after graduating from high school, where he served for three years. After leaving the Navy, he started his own record label and began emceeing locally. In 1987, Burrell recorded his first album, *Feel My Power*. His music, along with his dance moves, attracted the attention of Capitol Records. They offered him a recording contract and in 1988, he released the album *Let's Get It Started*.

Burrell is known as one of the pioneers of pop rap, a style of rap meant to appeal to a broad audience. Over his career, he recorded twelve albums. His third album, *Please Hammer, Don't Hurt Em'*, sold over 10 million copies, making it the first rap album to be certified diamond by the Recording Industry Association of America. In 1996, after poorly managing his finances, Burrell filed for bankruptcy. He has since made a comeback with successful careers in music, television, and business.

ARTIST SUMMARY

Artist/Group Name:

_____

Date and Place of Birth _or_ Where and When This Group Was Formed:

_____

_____

Famous Recordings:

_____

Reasons They Are Important to the history of Hip-Hop:

_____

_____

_____

_____

Interesting Facts:

_____

_____

_____

_____

HIP-HOP DURING THE 1980s — THE RISE OF POP RAP

What is pop rap and why did several original MCs dislike it? (2 points)

_____

_____

Why was *The Fresh Prince of Bel-Air* important to the history of hip-hop? (1 point)

_____

What song won *DJ Jazzy Jeff and Fresh Prince* a Grammy? (1 point)

_____

What is one film in which Will Smith has starred? (1 point)

_____

How did MC Hammer get his nickname? (1 point)

_____

Which MC Hammer album was certified platinum? (1 point)

_____

Where was MC Hammer born? (1 point)

_____

Using at least *two* sentences, describe why you like or dislike popular music. (2 points)

_____

_____

WORKSHEET (CONTINUED)

HIP-HOP DURING THE 1980s — THE RISE OF POP RAP

Will Smith has decided to make a comeback as a rapper (again). He wants your advice for what kind of music he should write. Should he continue writing pop rap or should he start writing music with a stronger message? Why? What kinds of topics should he write songs about? Why? (4 points)

_____

_____

_____

_____

_____

_____

_____

_____

_____

Rubric:

4 points	3 points	2 points	1 point	0 points
The response adequately answers all of the questions	The response adequately answers 3 of the questions	The response adequately answers 2 of the questions	The response adequately answers 1 of the questions	The response does not adequately answer any of the questions

Grading: 14 – 13 points = A, 12 – 11 points = B, 10 points = C, 9 points = D, 8 – 0 points= F

EVALUATION

HIP-HOP DURING THE 1980s — THE RISE OF POP RAP

Use the table below to rate how well you like the song being played. Give each aspect of the music a score from 1-5, with 5 indicating that you liked it a lot, and 1 indicating that you did not like it all. (1 point for each category completed)

Name of Song and Artist:

_____

Speed (Tempo)	
Changes in Volume (Dynamics)	
Lyrics/Message	
Sounds that are Used (Timbre/Instrumentation)	
Flow (Vocal Rhythms)	
Instrumental Rhythms/Beat	
Other:	
Total	

In your own words, describe what you think this song is about, who the intended audience is, and why using at least *three* sentences. (3 points)

_____

_____

_____

_____

Grading: 9 = A, 8 = B, 7 = C, 6 = D, 5-0 = F

COMPARE AND CONTRAST

HIP-HOP DURING THE 1980s — THE RISE OF POP RAP

Use the Venn diagram below to compare and contrast the songs played in class. Your Venn diagram must have a total of *ten* similarities and differences. Use the categories from your evaluation sheet (lyrics, speed, volume, sounds used, etc.) as a starting point. Only accurate descriptions will be counted. (10 points)

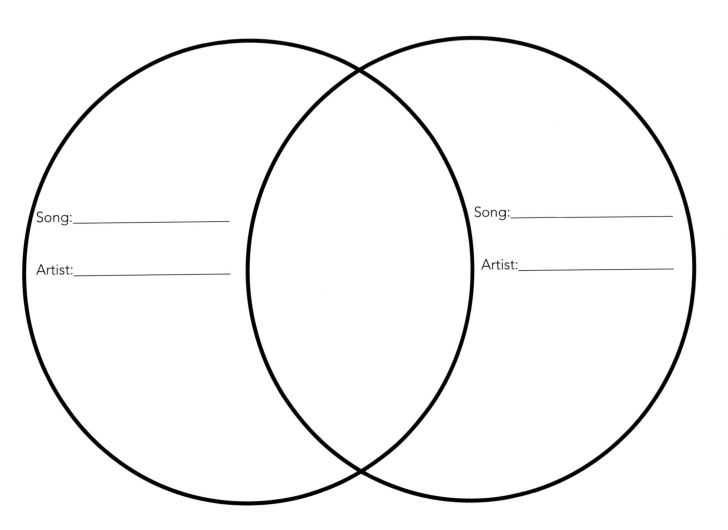

Song:_____

Artist:_____

Song:_____

Artist:_____

Grading: 10–9 points = A, 8 points = B, 7 points = C, 6 points = D, 5–0 points = F

SONG TOPICS

Use the space below to brainstorm song topics that appeal to many people and song topics that appeal to few people. In other words, what are some song topics that many people can relate to? What song topics could only a few people relate to?

Topics that Appeal to Many

Love, friendship, having fun, family, feeling lonely, feeling sad, feeling happy

_____

_____

_____

_____

_____

Topics that Appeal to Few

Religion, politics, race, violence, gender, age, substance abuse

_____

_____

_____

_____

_____

WORKSHEET ANSWER KEY

HIP-HOP DURING THE 1980S — THE RISE OF POP RAP

What is pop rap and why did several original MCs dislike it? (2 points)

Pop rap is music that has a message that connects to a large number of people. Original

MCs felt that pop rap's messages were too generic and that pop rap artists had sold out.

Why was *The Fresh Prince of Bel-Air* important to the history of hip-hop? (1 point)

It was the first show featuring a rapper –or- It showed that hip-hop had reached a new

level of popularity.

What song won DJ Jazzy Jeff and Fresh Prince a Grammy? (1 point)

Parents Just Don't Understand

What is one film in which Will Smith has starred? (1 point)

Men in Black; Bad Boys; Independence Day; Ali; I, Robot; Hancock; After Earth; etc.

How did MC Hammer get his nickname? (1 point)

Reggie Jackson called him "Hammer" because he looked like Hank Aaron.

Which MC Hammer album was certified platinum? (1 point)

Please Hammer, Don't Hurt 'Em

Where was MC Hammer born? (1 point)

Oakland, California

Using at least *two* sentences, describe why you like or dislike popular music. (2 points)

I like popular music because the backgrounds are fun to listen to. Also, the lyrics aren't

too serious.

WORKSHEET ANSWER KEY (CONTINUED)

HIP-HOP DURING THE 1980s — THE RISE OF POP RAP

Will Smith has decided to make a comeback as a rapper (again). He wants your advice for what kind of music he should write. Should he continue writing pop rap or should he start writing music with a stronger message? Why? What kinds of topics should he write songs about? Why? (4 points)

I think that he should keep writing pop rap. It is the best way to make money because

lots of people will buy it. He should write about relationships and what it's like to have a

family. Everybody can relate to those topics.

Rubric:

4 points	3 points	2 points	1 point	0 points
The response adequately answers all of the questions	The response adequately answers 3 of the questions	The response adequately answers 2 of the questions	The response adequately answers 1 of the questions	The response does not adequately answer any of the questions

Grading: 14 – 13 = A, 12 - 11 = B, 10 = C, 9 = D, 8 – 0 = F

COMPARE AND CONTRAST SAMPLE ANSWERS

HIP-HOP DURING THE 1980s — THE RISE OF POP RAP

Use the Venn diagram below to compare and contrast the songs played in class. Your Venn diagram must have a total of *ten* similarities and differences. Use the categories from your evaluation sheet (lyrics, speed, volume, sounds used, etc.) as a starting point. Only accurate descriptions will be counted. (10 points)

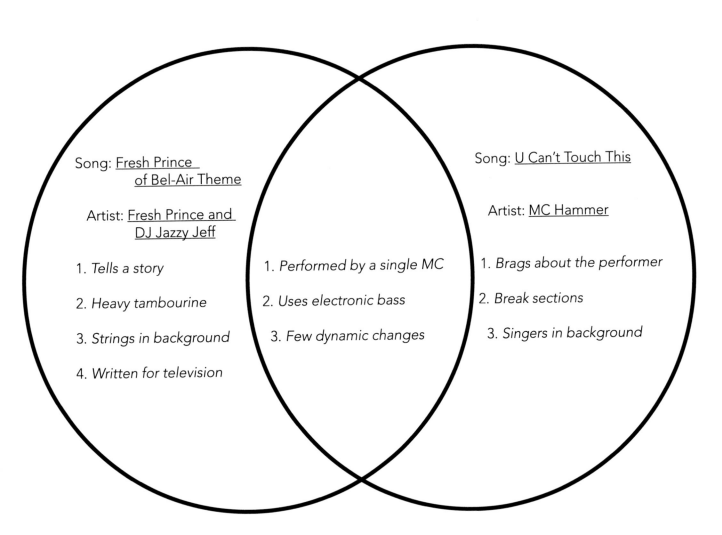

Song: <u>Fresh Prince of Bel-Air Theme</u>

Artist: <u>Fresh Prince and DJ Jazzy Jeff</u>

1. *Tells a story*

2. *Heavy tambourine*

3. *Strings in background*

4. *Written for television*

1. *Performed by a single MC*

2. *Uses electronic bass*

3. *Few dynamic changes*

Song: <u>U Can't Touch This</u>

Artist: <u>MC Hammer</u>

1. *Brags about the performer*

2. *Break sections*

3. *Singers in background*

Grading: 10-9 = A, 8 = B, 7 = C, 6 = D, 5-0 = F

LESSON

THE FRESH PRINCE OF BEL-AIR: HIP-HOP MEETS TELEVISION

Objectives:

- Students will reflect on hip-hop and its relationship to popular culture – Standard(s) 8, 9

Lesson Length: Approx. 50 min. (one class period)

Materials:

Pencil
Student Worksheet
The Fresh Prince of Bel-Air season 1, episode 1 (available for purchase on-line)

Procedures:

1. Have students look at *The Fresh Prince of Bel-Air* worksheet.

2. Read the following to students:
   "During the last class, you learned about pop rap. By the late 1980s hip-hop had become so popular that NBC created a television show starring a famous rapper. It was about a street-smart teenager from West Philadelphia who moves in with his wealthy aunt and uncle in Bel-Air. The show was called the Fresh Prince of Bel-Air. It starred Will Smith and aired from 1990 to 1996. The show was more than just a comedy. It dealt with several serious issues. Today you are going to watch the first episode in the series and answer some questions about some of the issues addressed by the show."

3. Play the *The Fresh Prince of Bel-Air* season 1, episode 1 and have students complete *The Fresh Prince of Bel-Air* worksheet.

4. Have students share their answers with a partner and then with the class.

Assessment:

The Fresh Prince of Bel-Air worksheet

WORKSHEET

THE FRESH PRINCE OF BEL-AIR

Background

The show *The Fresh Prince of Bel-Air* is more than just a television comedy. It deals with social issues that are as relevant today as they were when the show was written. The following questions are meant to help you identify and discuss those issues.

Question 1

Uncle Phil criticizes Will for using slang. Some believe that when young people use slang, adults cannot take them seriously. Others feel that slang represents an important part of who they are. What do you think about people who use slang? Do you use slang? Why? Are there situations where slang would be inappropriate? Are there situations where slang would be appropriate? (5 points)

_____

_____

_____

_____

_____

Question 2

When people think of discrimination, they often think of racism. However, Uncle Phil discriminates against Will because of his language, clothes, and attitude. Have you ever been treated differently because of the way that you look, dress, or speak? Explain. Have you ever treated another person differently because of the way that they look, dress, or speak? Why or why not? What are some things that people can do to end discrimination? (5 points)

_____

_____

_____

_____

Question 3

Will sees Uncle Phil as a man who has betrayed his African American heritage by the way that he lives and the friends that he has. How do you see Uncle Phil? Did the final scene where Uncle Phil talks about how he heard Malcolm X speak change how you think of him? Why or why not? (3 points)

_____

_____

_____

_____

Question 4

Uncle Phil sees Will as a young troublemaker from the streets. How do you see Will? Did the scene where Will plays Beethoven at the piano change how you think of him? Why or why not? (3 points)

_____

_____

_____

_____

Grading: 16–15 points = A, 14–13 points = B, 12 points = C, 11 – 10 points = D, 9–0 points = F

WORKSHEET SAMPLE ANSWERS

THE FRESH PRINCE OF BEL-AIR

Question 1

Uncle Phil criticizes Will for using slang. Some believe that when young people use slang adults cannot take them seriously. Others feel that slang represents an important part of who they are. What do you think about people who use slang? Do you use slang? Why? Are there situations where slang would be inappropriate? Are there situations where slang would be appropriate? (5 points)

I think that using slang isn't a big deal. I use some slang words. Sometimes they are the

best words for describing how I feel. Slang might be inappropriate in a job interview.

It is appropriate when you are around friends.

Question 2

When people think of discrimination they often think of racism. However, Uncle Phil discriminates against Will because of his language, clothes, and attitude. Have you ever been treated differently because of the way that you look, dress, or speak? Explain. Have you ever treated another person differently because of the way that they look, dress, or speak? Why or why not? What are some things that people can do to end discrimination? (5 points)

Yes, I have been treated differently because I wear glasses. I try not to discriminate but

sometimes I do. I know that I wouldn't want to be discriminated against so I do my best

not to. People can help end discrimination by getting to know people who are different

than they are.

Question 3

Will sees Uncle Phil as a man who has betrayed his African American heritage by the way that he lives and the friends that he has. How do you see Uncle Phil? Did the final scene where Uncle Phil talks about how he heard Malcolm X speak change how you think of him? -Why or why not? (3 points)

Uncle Phil is a person just like any other, who has worked hard to make money.

The scene where Uncle Phil shares his experiences with Malcolm X made me realize

that he helped make the world a place where African Americans can achieve the success

that he has.

Question 4

Uncle Phil sees Will as a young troublemaker from the streets. How do you see Will? Did the scene where Will plays Beethoven at the piano change how you think of him? Why or why not? (3 points)

I think that Will is a little bit of a troublemaker. The scene where Will plays the piano

made me realize that there may be more to him than he shows.

Grading: 16–15 points = A, 14–13 points = B, 12 points = C, 11–10 points = D, 9–0 points = F

LESSON

HIP-HOP DURING 1990s — THE RISE AND FALL OF GANG RAP

Objectives:
- Students will describe the lives and contributions of 2Pac and The Notorious B.I.G. to the history of hip-hop. – Standard(s) 9
- Students will evaluate and summarize hip-hop's impact on today's youth. – Standard(s) 8, 9
- Students will critically analyze an artist and their music. – Standard(s) 8, 9

Lesson Length: Approx. 90 min. (two classes)

Materials:
Pencils
Student Worksheets/Artist Summaries
Recording of "I'll Be Missing You" by Puff Daddy (optional)

Procedures:
1. Using the "Hip-Hop During 1990s – The Rise and Fall of Gang Rap Writing Prompt," give students five minutes to answer the following: What topics are today's hip-hop artists writing songs about? Do you like listening to music about these topics? Why or why not? If you don't, what kinds of songs do you enjoy listening to? Do you think that listening to music can affect how people act?

2. Have students share their answers with a partner and then with the class.

3. Read the following to students:
   "Pop rap's popularity decreased during the 1990s as gang rap's popularity grew. Music with gang themes had been around since the mid-1980s. However, by the 1990s, young listeners had taken to the controversial and often graphic lyrics. This concerned many adults. They worried that if young people listened to music that made illegal activities sound appealing, then they might be tempted to do those things themselves. Much of gang rap's popularity was due to the attention given to the East Coast/West Coast rivalry by the media. The rivalry centered around rappers from two record labels: Puff Daddy's New York-based Bad Boy Records and Suge Knight's California-based Death Row Records. The two most well-known rappers in the rivalry were 2Pac and The Notorious B.I.G.

   Though tensions had existed before, the feud between 2Pac and The Notorious B.I.G. began in 1994 when 2Pac was shot in the lobby of a Manhattan recording studio. He later blamed Puff Daddy and The Notorious B.I.G. for setting him up. Rappers from both coasts quickly took sides. Rappers began writing albums filled with taunts and insults directed towards the opposing group. Even though violence between the two groups was common, when an unidentified gunman murdered 2Pac in 1996 it shocked the country. Wallace was murdered a year later. They were twenty-five and twenty-four years old, respectively. After their deaths, a truce was called and gang rap eventually declined in popularity.

   Today you're going to read about 2Pac and The Notorious B.I.G., then discuss your thoughts about how music affects people your age."

4. Divide students into groups and have them read and complete summaries for either 2Pac or The Notorious B.I.G.

5. Have students share their summaries with the class and clarify as needed.

   You may choose to play "I'll Be Missing You" by Puff Daddy. Explain to them that this song was written by Puff Daddy after the death of his close friend, the Notorious B.I.G. The song is written as a message to the Notorious B.I.G. letting him know how much he is loved and missed. It samples the Police's "Every Breath You Take."

   **If you choose to play this song, be advised that the introduction contains profanity. Beginning after the introduction is recommended.

6. In pairs, have students complete the "Hip-Hop During 1990s – The Rise and Fall of Gang Rap Worksheet."

7. Read the following to students:
   "You read earlier that adults were concerned about the influence that gang rap might have on young people. Today you are going to have a chance to share your thoughts and opinions about how music influences people your age."

8. Lead the students in a class discussion about the influence that hip-hop has on people their age. The following questions can serve as a guide for leading the discussion:
   * Have students share their answers from the beginning of class.
   * Is hip-hop a positive or negative influence on people your age? Can it be both? Why?
   * Who listens to hip-hop?
   * How do you think girls feel about the way that many rappers talk about them?
   * What kinds of things do songs on the radio talk about?
   * How do you feel about what rappers rap about?
   * What are some things that you like about hip-hop?
   * What are some things that you dislike about hip-hop?
   * Do you want to be like the rappers that you see on TV and hear on the radio? Why or why not?
   * How would you respond to someone who says that young people should not be allowed to listen to music with controversial lyrics?
   * What would you like to hear rappers rap about?
   * What changes would you like to see in rap music, if any? Is there anything that you can do to make those changes happen?
   * Do you think that artists should change their music because it may offend some people? Why or why not?

9. Using the "Hip-Hop During 1990s – The Rise and Fall of Gang Rap Letter Template," have students write a letter to a famous artists summarizing their opinion about the artist's music.

   *If you would like to send your students' letters to the artists, many artists have fan mail addresses available on their websites.

Assessment:
Hip-Hop During 1990s – The Rise and Fall of Gang Rap Worksheet
Letters to Artists

WRITING PROMPT

HIP-HOP DURING THE 1990s — THE RISE AND FALL OF GANG RAP

In the space below, answer the following: What topics are today's hip-hop artists writing songs about? Do you like listening to music about these topics? Why or why not? If you don't, what kinds of songs do you enjoy listening to? Do you think that listening to music can affect how people act? If yes, give an example.

_____

_____

_____

_____

_____

_____

_____

_____

_____

_____

_____

_____

_____

artist profile

Tupac Shakur was born in 1971 in New York but later moved to Marin City, California. As a youth, he studied the arts extensively, including theater, dance, and poetry. At the age of nineteen, he joined California-based rap group Digital Underground as a roadie and dancer. After making several appearances as a rapper with Digital Underground, he released his first solo album *2Pacalypse Now*. Shakur signed with Death Row Records in 1995 when, after serving eleven months of a prison sentence, Death Row's CEO, Suge Knight, posted his $1.4 million bail. In addition to his recording career, he is known for his feud with Christopher "The Notorious B.I.G." Wallace that brought

considerable attention to the East Coast/West Coast rivalry.

The feud between Shakur and Wallace began in 1994 when Shakur was shot multiple times in the lobby of a Manhattan

recording studio. He later blamed Sean "Puff Daddy" Combs and Wallace for setting him up. Rappers from both coasts quickly took sides. What followed was a flood of albums filled with taunts and insults directed towards the opposing group. Though violent outbursts between factions were common, when an unidentified gunman murdered Shakur in 1996, the entire country took notice. Wallace was murdered a year later in a similar fashion. They were twenty-five and twenty-four years old, respectively. After their deaths, a truce was called followed by a decline in the presence of gang rap.

artist profile

THE NOTORIOUS B.I.G.

Christopher Wallace, better known as "the Notorious B.I.G." or "Biggie Smalls," was born in 1972 in the Bronx. He became involved in crime at a young age and by the time that he was twenty years old, he had been arrested multiple times. Rapping had been a part of his life since he was a teenager and after being featured in *Source* Magazine's Unsigned Hype column, he was signed to Uptown Records in 1992. He quickly left, however, to sign with newly formed Bad Boy Records. Wallace became close friends with Bad Boy founder and CEO Sean Combs. In addition to his recording career, he is known for his feud with Tupac Shakur that brought considerable attention to the East Coast/ West Coast rivalry.

The feud between Shakur and Wallace began in 1994 when Shakur was shot multiple times in the lobby of a Manhattan recording studio. He later blamed Combs and Wallace for setting him up. Rappers from both coasts quickly took sides. What followed was a flood of albums filled with taunts and insults directed towards the opposing group. Though violent outbursts between factions were common, when an unidentified gunman murdered Shakur in 1996, the entire country took notice. Wallace was murdered a year later in a similar fashion. They were twenty-five and twenty-four years old, respectively.

After their deaths, a truce was called followed by a decline in the presence of gang rap.

ARTIST SUMMARY

Artist/Group Name:

_____

Date and Place of Birth _or_ Where and When This Group Was Formed:

_____

_____

Famous Recordings:

_____

Reasons They Are Important to the history of Hip-Hop:

_____

_____

_____

_____

Interesting Facts:

_____

_____

_____

_____

WORKSHEET

HIP-HOP DURING THE 1990S — THE RISE AND FALL OF GANG RAP

What was the East Coast/West Coast rivalry and who were the people involved? (2 points)

_____

_____

_____

What record companies were involved in the East Coast/West Coast rivalry? (2 points)

_____

_____

Why were many adults concerned about gang rap? (1 point)

_____

_____

What rap group did Tupac work with before he recorded as a solo artist? (1 point)

_____

Where was The Notorious B.I.G. born? (1 point)

_____

What is The Notorious B.I.G.'s real name? (1 point)

_____

How old were Tupac and The Notorious B.I.G. when they died? (2 points)

_____

_____

HIP-HOP DURING THE 1990s — THE RISE AND FALL OF GANG RAP

Imagine that you are able to go back in time and speak with Tupac and The Notorious B.I.G. when they were children. Would you encourage them to do anything differently with their lives? Why or why not? If you would encourage them to do something differently, what would it be? Why? (2 points)

_____

_____

_____

Imagine that you are an original MC from the 1970s who is living during the 1990s. How do you feel about gang rap? How has hip-hop changed from the 1970s? (2 points)

_____

_____

_____

Imagine that you are a parent during the 1990s. Would you let your children listen to gang rap? Why or why not? (2 points)

_____

_____

_____

Rubric for each question:

2 points	1 point	0 points
The response adequately answers all of the questions	The response adequately answers 1 of the questions	The response does not adequately answer any of the questions

Grading: 16 – 15 points = A, 14 – 13 points = B, 12 points = C, 11 – 10 points = D, 9 – 0 points = F

LETTER TEMPLATE

HIP-HOP DURING THE 1990S — THE RISE AND FALL OF GANG RAP

Choose an artist whose music you are familiar with. Use the guide below to write them a letter telling them what you think about their music and their influence on people your age. In your letter be sure to include the following:

- What you like about their music, if anything, and why
- What you don't like about their music, if anything, and why
- How they influence young people
- What you think they should do differently, if anything and why

Dear _____,

    My name is _____ and I am writing to you

because_____

_____

_____

_____

_____

_____

_____

_____

_____

_____

_____

_____

_____

_____

_____

_____

_____

_____

_____

_____

_____

Thank you for your time.

Sincerely,

_____

Rubric:

A	B	C	D	F
The response adequately answers all of the questions	The response adequately answers 3 of the questions	The response adequately answers 2 of the questions	The response adequately answers 1 of the questions	The response does not adequately answer any of the questions

WORKSHEET ANSWER KEY

HIP-HOP DURING THE 1990s — THE RISE AND FALL OF GANG RAP

What was the East Coast/West Coast rivalry and who were two people involved? (2 points)

The East Coast/West Coast rivalry was a feud between rappers from the east and west

coasts of the country, specifically New York and California. 2Pac and The Notorious

B.I.G. were two of the main people involved.

What record companies were involved in the East Coast/West Coast rivalry? (2 points)

Bad Boy Records and Death Row Records

Why were many adults concerned about gang rap? (1 point)

They were afraid that young people would be encouraged to do the things that many

rappers talked about.

What rap group did 2Pac work with before he recorded as a solo artist? (1 point)

Digital Underground

Where was The Notorious B.I.G. born? (1 point)

The Bronx area of New York City

What is The Notorious B.I.G.'s real name? (1 point)

Christopher Wallace

How old were 2Pac and The Notorious B.I.G. when they died? (2 points)

2Pac was 25 and The Notorious B.I.G. was 24

HIP-HOP DURING THE 1990s — THE RISE AND FALL OF GANG RAP

Imagine that you are able to go back in time and speak with 2Pac and The Notorious B.I.G. when they were children. Would you encourage them to do anything differently with their lives? Why or why not? If you would encourage them to do something differently, what would it be? Why? (2 points)

I would encourage them to stay away from gangs so that they could have stayed out of

trouble and lived longer. I would tell them to use their music to inspire people to do

great things so that the world would be a better place.

Imagine that you are an original MC from the 1970s who is living during the 1990s. How do you feel about gang rap? How has hip-hop changed from the 1970s? (2 points)

I feel that gang rap is misrepresenting hip-hop. When we started MCing, the music

was about having fun and making our world better.

Imagine that you are a parent during the 1990s. Would you let your children listen to gang rap? Why or why not? (2 points)

I would not let my children listen to gang rap because I'd be afraid that they would

be encouraged to do bad things.

Rubric for each question:

2 points	1 point	0 points
The response adequately answers all of the questions	The response adequately answers 1 of the questions	The response does not adequately answer any of the questions

Grading: 16 – 15 points = A, 14 – 13 points = B, 12 points = C, 11 – 10 points = D, 9 – 0 points = F

LETTER MODEL RESPONSE

HIP-HOP DURING THE 1990s — THE RISE AND FALL OF GANG RAP

Choose an artist whose music you are familiar with. Use the guide below to write them a letter telling them what you think about their music and their influence on people your age. In your letter be sure to include the following:

- What you like about their music, if anything, and why
- What you don't like about their music, if anything, and why
- How they influence young people
- What you think they should do differently, if anything and why

Dear _Eminem,_

My name is _Robert Vagi_ and I am writing to you because _I would like to tell you_

about how your music affects people my age. I really like the fact that you write songs

about real life because it can help others get through their own problems. However,

I think that when you curse and use such graphic language that it encourages other

people to do it, too. Your music may help people my age deal with their problems,

but it also encourages them to use language that is inappropriate. I would like it if you

could write some music with clean, expressive lyrics that encourage people to do great

things.

Thank you for your time.

Sincerely,

Robert Vagi

Rubric:

A	B	C	D	F
The response adequately answers all of the questions	The response adequately answers 3 of the questions	The response adequately answers 2 of the questions	The response adequately answers 1 of the questions	The response does not adequately answer any of the questions

Lesson

WOMEN IN HIP-HOP

Objectives:

- Students will summarize the lives of Queen Latifah, Lauryn Hill, and Salt-N-Pepa and their contributions to the history of hip-hop – Standard(s) 8, 9
- Students will analyze and evaluate a hip-hop song – Standard(s) 6, 7
- Students will analyze, evaluate, compare, and contrast a song and its hip-hop cover – Standard(s) 6, 7, 9

Lesson Length: Approx. 90 min. (two classes)

Materials:
Pencils
Student Worksheets/Artist Summaries
Recordings of the following:

- "Killing Me Softly With His Song" by Lauryn Hill and The Fugees
- "Killing Me Softly With His Song" by Roberta Flack
- "Dance for Me" by Queen Latifah

Procedures:

1. Using the "Women in Hip-Hop Opening Activity," give students five minutes to write down as many male and female hip-hop artists as they can.
2. Have students share their answers with a partner, then with the class.
3. Create a class list and point out the disproportionate number of men and women.
4. Read the following to students:
   "Since hip-hop began, most artists have been men. There have, however, been many successful female artists. Today you are going to learn about a few of them."
5. Divide students into three groups and have each group read and complete summaries for the following artists: Queen Latifah, Lauryn Hill, Salt-N-Pepa.
6. Have students share their summaries with the class and clarify as needed.
7. Divide students into groups of three and have them complete the Women in Hip-Hop worksheet. Each group should consist of one representative from each of the previous groups.
8. Read the following to students:
   "You read earlier about Queen Latifah. I'm going to play her song "Dance for Me" from her first album, All Hail the Queen."
9. Have students fill out a "Women in Hip-Hop Evaluation Sheet."
10. Have students share their answers with a partner and then with the class.
11. Read the following to students:
    "You also read about Lauryn Hill. She became famous as both a singer and a rapper. Her cover of Roberta Flack's "Killing Me Softly With His Song" brought her to the public's attention. When an artist covers another artist's song, they make it his or her own. I am going to play Roberta Flack's version of "Killing Me Softly With His Song" followed by Lauryn Hill's version."
12. Have students complete a "Women in Hip-Hop Evaluation Sheet" for each song.
13. Have students share their answers with each other and then the class.
14. Play both versions of "Killing Me Softly" and have students complete the "Women in Hip-Hop Compare and Contrast" worksheet.
15. Have students share their answers with the class and create a class Venn diagram.

Assessment:
Women in Hip-Hop Worksheets
Women in Hip-Hop Evaluation Sheets
Women in Hip-Hop Compare and Contrast Sheet
Venn Diagram

WOMEN IN HIP-HOP OPENING ACTIVITY

In the space below, write down the names of as many male rappers and as many female rappers as you can.

Male Rappers

_____

_____

_____

_____

_____

_____

Female Rappers

_____

_____

_____

_____

_____

artist profile

QUEEN LATIFAH

Dana Elaine Owens, commonly known as "Queen Latifah," was born in 1970 and raised in East Orange, New Jersey. She was given her nickname "Latifah" when she was eight, by her cousin. It means "gentle" in Arabic. She began her musical career as a beatboxer (someone who makes percussive sounds with their mouth). After working as an MC, she gained the attention of Tommy Boy Records and released her first single "Wrath of My Madness" in 1988. In 1989, she released her first full album, *All Hail the Queen*. Between 1989 and 1998, she released four hip-hop albums. In 2004, Owens released her fifth album *The Dana Owens Album*. This recording marked a shift in her career. Though she had sung on many of her hip-hop recordings, *The Dana Owens Album* consisted largely of her singing jazz standards. She has continued her music career as both a singer and rapper. She is one of hip-hop's most successful female artists.

gdcgraphics [CC-BY-SA-2.0 (http://creativecommons.org/licenses/by-sa/2.0)], via Wikimedia Commons

Like many other hip-hop artists, Owens has had success outside of music. She began her acting career in 1993 on the sitcom *Living Single* and went on to star in films like *Chicago* and *Hairspray*. Owens has also had success as a model and spokesperson for companies like COVERGIRL and Jenny Craig.

artist profile

Lauryn Hill was born in 1975 in East Orange, New Jersey. She was raised in a musical family. During high school, Prakazrel "Pras" Michel approached her about forming a musical group. She agreed and along with Michel's cousin, Wyclef Jean, they formed *The Fugees*. Both Michel and Jean were Haitian and chose the name as a reference to the term "refugee," a person who has left their country to escape danger or persecution. *The Fugees* went on to become international stars. Their most successful album, *The Score*, had several hits, one of them being a cover of Roberta Flack's "Killing Me Softly With His Song," featuring Lauryn Hill as the lead vocalist. In 1993, she played a leading role the film *Sister Act II*, where her singing was central to the film. In 1998, she released her first solo album, *The Miseducation of Lauryn Hill*. It featured Hill as both a rapper and singer. The album was incredibly successful and eventually earned her

five Grammys, making her the first female artist to receive so many in one evening. After the success of *The Miseducation of Lauryn Hill*, Hill chose to avoid publicity. Through the early 2000s she recorded sporadically and made occasional public appearances. She has become known for her social activism and charity work.

artist profile

Salt-N-Pepa is a hip-hop trio who formed in 1985. The group was originally from Queens, New York and consisted of Cheryl "Salt" James, Sandra "Pepa" Denton, and Deidra "DJ Spinderella" Roper. Under their original name *Super Nature*, they released their first single "The Showstopper" in 1985. It was successful enough to gain the attention of Next Plateau Records. In 1986, they signed with Next Plateau and released their first full-length album, *Hot, Cool, and Vicious*. Salt-N-Pepa continued to record albums and in 1995 won a Grammy Award in the Best Rap Performance category for their single "None of Your Business." This made them the first female rappers to win a Grammy Award. Between 1986 and 1997, Salt-N-Pepa recorded five albums. They officially disbanded in 2002. Many of their albums have been certified either platinum or gold.

ARTIST SUMMARY

Artist/Group Name:

_____

Date and Place of Birth _or_ Where and When This Group Was Formed:

_____

_____

Famous Recordings:

_____

Reasons they are important to the history of Hip-Hop:

_____

_____

_____

Interesting Facts:

_____

_____

_____

_____

_____

WORKSHEET

WOMEN IN HIP-HOP

What is Queen Latifah's real name? (1 point)

_____

What does Latifah mean in Arabic? (1 point)

_____

What are two ways that Queen Latifah's career has changed since she started? (2 points)

_____

What was the name of Lauryn Hill's first musical group and where did their name come from? (2 points)

_____

What movie featured Lauryn Hill? (1 point)

_____

What album won five Grammys for Lauryn Hill? (1 point)

_____

In which category did Salt-N-Pepa win a Grammy? (1 point)

_____

Where were Salt-N-Pepa originally from? (1 point)

_____

Why do you think that there are fewer females in hip-hop than men? (1 point)

_____

WORKSHEET (CONTINUED)

WOMEN IN HIP-HOP

Imagine that you are a famous MC during the 1980s. A young lady approaches you and asks for advice about how she can become an MC. What steps should she take? Will it be harder for her to be a successful MC because she is a woman? If so, why? (2 points)

_____

_____

_____

_____

Imagine that you are a female MC. How does performing in a musical style where most artists are men make you feel? Do you have to change anything about yourself to be successful? If so, what do you have to change? Do you think that this is right? (2 points)

_____

_____

_____

_____

Rubric for each question:

2 points	1 point	0 points
The response adequately answers all of the questions	The response adequately answers 1 of the questions	The response does not adequately answer any of the questions

Grading: 15 – 14 points = A, 13 – 12 points = B, 11 points = C, 10 – 9 points = D, 8 – 0 points = F

EVALUATION

WOMEN IN HIP-HOP

Use the table below to rate how well you like the song being played. Give each aspect of the music a score from 1–5, with 5 indicating that you liked it a lot and 1 indicating that you did not like it all. (1 point for each category completed)

Name of Song and Artist:

_____

Speed (Tempo)	
Changes in Volume (Dynamics)	
Lyrics/Message	
Sounds that are Used (Timbre/Instrumentation)	
Flow (Vocal Rhythms)	
Instrumental Rhythms/Beat	
Other:	
Total	

In your own words, describe what you think this song is about, who the intended audience is, and why using at least *three* sentences. (3 points)

_____

_____

_____

_____

Grading: 9 = A, 8 = B, 7 = C, 6 = D, 5-0 = F

COMPARE AND CONTRAST

WOMEN IN HIP-HOP

Use the Venn diagram below to compare and contrast the songs played in class. Your Venn diagram must have a total of *ten* similarities and differences. Use the categories from your evaluation sheet (lyrics, speed, volume, sounds used, etc.) as a starting point. Only accurate descriptions will be counted. (10 points)

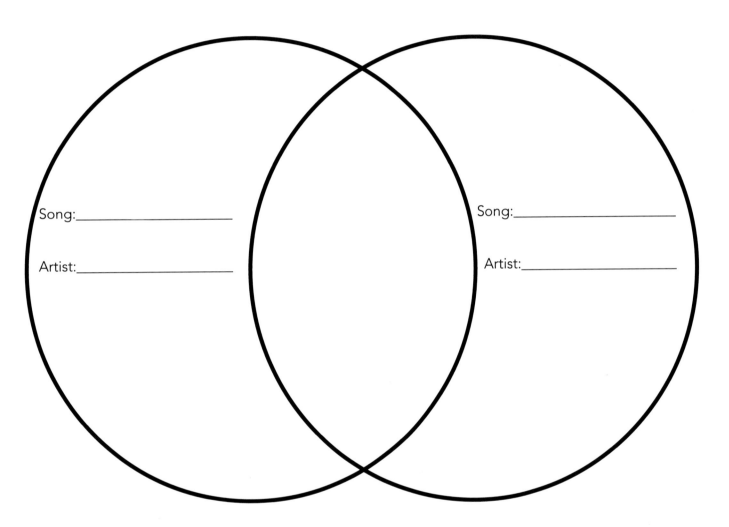

Song:_____

Artist:_____

Song:_____

Artist:_____

Grading: 10 points = A, 9 points = B, 8 points = C, 7 points = D, 6-0 points = F

ANSWER KEY

WOMEN IN HIP-HOP WORKSHEET

What is Queen Latifah's real name? (1 point)

Dana Owens

What does "Latifah" mean in Arabic? (1 point)

Gentle

What are two ways that Queen Latifah's career has changed since she started? (2 points)

She has started singing jazz music and acting.

What was the name of Lauryn Hill's first musical group and where did their name come from? (2 points)

Lauryn Hill was a member of the Fugees, which is short for "refugee."

What movie featured Lauryn Hill? (1 point)

Sister Act II

What album won five Grammys for Lauryn Hill? (1 point)

The Miseducation of Lauryn Hill

What category did Salt-N-Pepa win a Grammy in? (1 point)

Best Rap Performance

Where were Salt-N-Pepa originally from? (1 point)

Queens, New York

Why do you think that there are fewer females in hip-hop than men? (1 point)

I think that there are fewer women because men control the music business.

ANSWER KEY (CONTINUED)
WOMEN IN HIP-HOP WORKSHEET

Imagine that you are a famous MC during the 1980s. A young lady approaches you and asks for advice about how she can become an MC. What steps should she take? Will it be harder for her to be a successful MC because she is a woman? If so, why? (2 points)

I would tell her that she should try to start performing as often as possible. Also, she

should try to make lots of contacts. If she is a good MC, the fact that she's a woman

won't matter.

Imagine that you are a female MC. How does performing in a musical style where most artists are men make you feel? Do you have to change anything about yourself to be successful? If so, what do you have to change? (2 points)

It makes me feel lonely and like there is extra pressure for me to do well. I feel like I

either have to dress more provocatively or act tougher so that I can get noticed.

Rubric for each question:

2 points	1 point	0 points
The response adequately answers all of the questions	The response adequately answers 1 of the questions	The response does not adequately answer any of the questions

Grading: 15 – 14 points = A, 13 – 12 points = B, 11 points = C, 10 – 9 points = D, 8 – 0 points = F

COMPARE AND CONTRAST SAMPLE ANSWERS

WOMEN IN HIP-HOP

Use the Venn diagram below to compare and contrast the songs played in class. Your Venn diagram must have a total of *ten* similarities and differences. Use the categories from your evaluation sheet (lyrics, speed, volume, sounds used, etc.) as a starting point. Only accurate descriptions will be counted. (10 points)

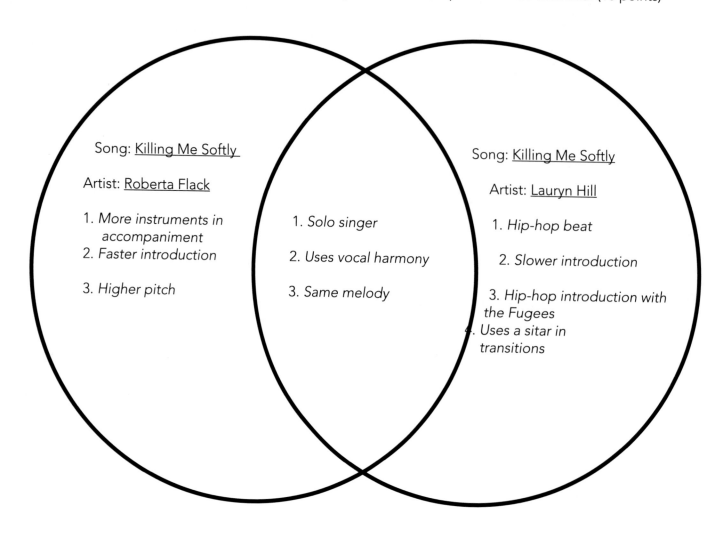

Song: <u>Killing Me Softly</u>

Artist: <u>Roberta Flack</u>

1. *More instruments in accompaniment*
2. *Faster introduction*

3. *Higher pitch*

1. *Solo singer*

2. *Uses vocal harmony*

3. *Same melody*

Song: <u>Killing Me Softly</u>

Artist: <u>Lauryn Hill</u>

1. *Hip-hop beat*

2. *Slower introduction*

3. *Hip-hop introduction with the Fugees*
4. *Uses a sitar in transitions*

Grading: 10 points = A, 9 points = B, 8 points = C, 7 points = D, 6-0 points = F

Hɪᴘ-Hᴏᴘ Hɪsᴛᴏʀʏ

Fɪɴᴀʟ Exᴀᴍ

Using the blank timeline below, describe what happened in the history of hip-hop during each decade, using at least *two* sentences. Also, name at least two artists who were either recording or performing during that time. (4 points per decade)

1970s

Description:

Artists:
1.

2.

1980s

Description:

Artists:
1.

2.

1990s

Description:

Artists:

1.

2.

When and where did hip-hop begin? (2 points)

_____

In at least _five_ sentences, describe how hip-hop, break dancing, and rapping began.
(5 points)

_____

_____

_____

_____

_____

Hip-Hop History (continued)

Final Exam

What was the title of the first rap song ever released to the public? When was it released?
Who recorded it? Why was it controversial? (4 points)

_____

_____

_____

_____

_____

Using at least *two* sentences, describe how RUN-DMC changed hip-hop. (2 points)

_____

_____

What is pop rap? Name one pop rapper. (2 points)

_____

_____

What was the East Coast/West Coast rivalry? Name two artists who were involved. How did it end?
(4 points)

_____

_____

_____

_____

HIP-HOP HISTORY (CONTINUED)

FINAL EXAM

How do you feel that hip-hop today influences young people? Is it good, bad, or both? Give an example. If you could change anything about hip-hop, would you? Why or why not? If you would change something, what would it be? (5 points)

_____

_____

_____

_____

_____

_____

_____

_____

_____

_____

Rubric:

5 points	4 points	3 points	2 points	1 point	0 points
The response adequately answers five questions	The response adequately answers four questions	The response adequately answers three questions	The response adequately answers two questions	The response adequately answers one question	The response does not adequately answer any questions

HIP-HOP HISTORY

FINAL EXAM
(CONTINUED)

"Young people should not be allowed to listen to music with explicit or controversial lyrics." Do you agree or disagree? Give two reasons for your opinion. (3 points)

_____

_____

_____

_____

_____

_____

_____

_____

_____

Rubric:

3 points	2 points	1 point	0 points
The response adequately answers three questions	The response adequately answers two questions	The response adequately answers one question	The response does not adequately answer any questions

Grading: 38 – 35 points = A, 34 – 31 points = B, 30 – 27 points = C, 26 – 23 points = D, 22 – 0 points = F

ANSWER KEY

HIP-HOP HISTORY FINAL EXAM

Using the blank timeline below, describe what happened in the history of hip-hop during each decade using at least *two* sentences. Also, name at least two artists who were either recording or performing during that time. (4 points per decade)

1970s

Description:
Hip-hop began as a series of dance parties in the Bronx. During that time, break dancing and rapping developed.

Artists:
1. *Kool Herc*

2. *Grandmaster Flash*

1980s

Description:
Hip-hop entered the mainstream recording industry and grew in popularity. Because public demand for hip-hop increased, a style of rap music developed, called pop rap.

Artists:
1. *Kurtis Blow*

2. *RUN-DMC*

1990s

Description:
Pop rap decreased in popularity and gang rap's popularity increased. The deaths of 2Pac and The Notorious B.I.G. brought about the end of the East Coast/West Coast rivalry.

Artists:
1. *2Pac*

2. *Lauryn Hill*

Where did hip-hop begin? In what year did "the birth of hip-hop" occur? (2 points)

1973 in the Bronx area of New York City

In at least *five* sentences, describe how hip-hop, break dancing, and rapping began.
(5 points)

In 1973 Kool Herc threw a dance party in the Bronx. It was so popular, that other DJs

started throwing their own parties. People would dance competitively at these parties

during instrumental breaks. This kind of competitive dancing became known as break

dancing. There were also MCs at many of the dance parties, who introduced the DJ and

riled up the crowd. MCs began including elaborate rhymes. This became rapping.

HIP-HOP HISTORY FINAL EXAM
(CONTINUED)

What was the title of the first rap song ever released to the public? When was it released? Who recorded it? Why was it controversial? (4 points)

The first song ever released to the public was "Rapper's Delight" by the Sugarhill Gang.

It was released in 1979. It was controversial because the members of the Sugarhill

Gang were not well-known MCs and some of their lyrics were taken from Grandmaster Caz.

Using at least *two* sentences, describe how RUN-DMC changed hip-hop. (2 points)

RUN-DMC used a beat machine to create heavier backgrounds. Their image was also

edgier than earlier artists.

What is pop rap? Name one pop rapper. (2 points)

Pop rap is music that is meant to be liked by a large number of people. Fresh Prince

recorded pop rap.

What was the East Coast/West Coast rivalry? Name two artists who were involved. How did it end? (4 points)

The East Coast/West Coast rivalry was a dispute between rappers from east coast

and west coast record labels. 2Pac and The Notorious B.I.G. were involved. It ended

when a truce was called following the deaths of 2Pac and the Notorious B.I.G.

ANSWER KEY

HIP-HOP HISTORY FINAL EXAM
(CONTINUED)

How do you feel that hip-hop today influences young people? (Is it good, bad, or both?) Give an example. If you could change anything about hip-hop, would you? Why or why not? If you would change something, what would it be? (4 points)

I feel that hip-hop is both a positive and negative influence on young people. It can

encourage men to treat women poorly but it can also inspire them to strive to succeed in

life. I would change the fact that rappers write music that speaks poorly about women.

I would do this so that men who listen to hip-hop would treat women better.

Rubric:

4 points	3 points	2 points	1 point	0 points
The response adequately answers four questions	The response adequately answers three questions	The response adequately answers two questions	The response adequately answers one question	The response does not adequately answer any questions

HIP-HOP HISTORY FINAL EXAM
(CONTINUED)

"Young people should not be allowed to listen to music with explicit or controversial lyrics." Do you agree or disagree? Give two reasons for your opinion. (3 points)

I disagree. I feel that we have the right to listen to whatever music we want to. People

can choose to ignore the parts of the music that they find offensive.

Rubric:

3 points	2 points	1 point	0 points
The response adequately answers three questions	The response adequately answers two questions	The response adequately answers one question	The response does not adequately answer any questions

Grading: 38 – 35 points = A, 34 – 31 points = B, 30 – 27 points = C, 26 – 23 points = D, 22 – 0 points = F

HIP-HOP HISTORY

INTERVIEW PROJECT

The purpose of this project is to allow you to learn about early hip-hop history from the perspective of someone who lived through it. Find someone who was alive during the 1970s and 1980s and who listened to hip-hop during that time. Ask them the following questions and write down their answers. Be prepared to share them with your class.

What was your first impression of hip-hop?

_____

_____

_____

_____

_____

How did adults feel about hip-hop when it first came out?

_____

_____

_____

_____

_____

How did hip-hop artists dress?

_____

_____

_____

_____

_____

HIP-HOP HISTORY

INTERVIEW
(CONTINUED)

Did you know any MC's, DJ's, or break-dancers? If so, can you describe them?

_____

_____

_____

_____

_____

_____

What do you think about today's hip-hop?

_____

_____

_____

_____

_____

_____

Do you have any interesting stories about hip-hop that you would like to share?

_____

_____

_____

_____

_____

_____

SONGWRITING

LESSON

CLASS SONG

Objectives:
- Students will compose two verses and a hook describing their school – Standard(s) 4
- Students will perform their class composition – Standard(s) 1

Lesson Length: Approx. 90 min. (two class periods)

Materials:
Pencils
Copies of Student Worksheets
Paper for Brainstorming
Whiteboard/Marker
Fresh Beats CD

Procedure:
1. Begin by copying the "Class Song Worksheet" onto the board.
2. Explain to students that as a class they are going to write a song about their school.
3. Ask students to take out the "Class Song Worksheet."
4. In pairs, have students create sentences that introduce their school. They should write these sentences on a separate sheet of paper.
5. Listen to students' sentences and choose one that can easily be recited rhythmically in four beats.

   Good Example: We're here at Murphy and we're an A school.
                    1   2   3   4
   Bad Example: We're here at Murphy and we like to learn lots of things.
                 1   2   3   4   5
   Bad Example: We like it here at Murphy.
              1   2   3

   * You can change the rhythm of words to fit into as many beats as you like. However, those that fall into four beats naturally are easiest to work with.

6. Once you've chosen a sentence, write it on the first line of the "Introduce Your School" bracket. Have students do the same on their worksheets.
7. Point out the last word of the first line to students. Have students, in pairs, brainstorm words that rhyme with the last word of the first line.
8. Have students share their words with the class. Create a class list of rhyming words.

   Example: First Line: "We're here at Murphy and we're an A school."
          Rhyming Words: cool, pool, tool, stool, mule, etc.

9. In pairs, have students brainstorm sentences that relate to the first sentence and end with one of the rhyming words. Again, students should do this on a separate sheet of paper.

   Example: "We're here at Murphy and we're an A school."
          1   2   3   4
          "We work really hard and we think that's cool."
          1   2   3   4

10. Have groups share their sentences with the class.
11. After listening to students' answers, choose a sentence that fits into four beats and write it underneath of the first line. Have students do the same on their worksheets.
12. Play one of the backgrounds from the *Fresh Beats* CD and have students practice reciting the first two lines as a class.

When students recite rap lyrics, the words should be spoken rhythmically. It may help to explain to students that their words should "sound like a drum." In other words, someone should be able to dictate the rhythm of their words.

13. Repeat this process for each of the brackets on the "Class Song Worksheet." Complete verses 1 and 2. Do *not* complete the "Hook" section.
14. Read the following to students:

"Each set of eight lines that you composed is called a verse. A verse is a section of a song that has similar music but different words. We are now going to write our hook. Most popular music is written in what is called verse-chorus form. A song's form describes how it is pieced together. A song in verse-chorus form is made up of verses (sections with similar music but different words) with a chorus in between each verse. The chorus is a section that repeats throughout the song and often summarizes its message. The chorus is the same every time and is usually the section that people remember. However, in hip-hop the chorus is called the hook."

11. Ask students, with their partners, to compose two lines that summarize the song. Again, students should use a separate sheet of paper.

If students struggle with this, have the first line be the school's name spelled out.

Example: "M – U – R – P – H – Y"
        1   2 3   4
    "We work hard so our dreams can fly.
     1   2   3   4

12. Have students share their answers with the class.
13. Choose a hook and write it in the corresponding bracket. Have students do the same in their workbooks.
14. Practice the entire song.

CLASS SONG WORKSHEET

Use the following worksheet to complete your class song. For every bracket, you will write two lines about the topic that is listed. Each pair of lines should end with rhyming words. Also, you should be able to recite each line and have it fit into four beats.

Introduce your school.

_____

_____

Tell where your school is located.

V
E _____
R
S _____
E

1 *Describe what happens at your school.*

_____

_____

Describe the students at your school.

_____

_____

HOOK

_____

_____

CLASS SONG WORKSHEET
(Continued)

Describe a teacher that you like.

_____

_____

Describe a teacher that you like.

V
E
R
S
E

_____

_____

Describe a teacher that you like.

2

_____

_____

Describe your principal.

_____

_____

HOOK

_____

_____

CLASS SONG MODEL RESPONSE

Use the following worksheet to complete your class song. For every bracket you will write two lines about the topic that is listed. Each pair of lines should end with rhyming words. Also, you should be able to recite each line and have it fit into four beats.

Introduce your school.

We're here at Murphy and we're an A school.

We work really hard and we think that's cool.

Tell where your school is located.

Our school's out here in west AZ.

We love our school 'cause it's the place to be.

Describe what happens at your school.

All day we fill our brains with lots of knowledge.

Workin' real hard so we can to get to college.

Describe the students at your school.

Our students are the best in the state.

Everyone works hard to be great.

VERSE 1

HOOK

M – U – R – P – H – Y

We work hard so our dreams can fly.

CLASS SONG MODEL RESPONSE
(CONTINUED)

Describe a teacher that you like.

V E R S E 2

We like Mrs. K. 'cause she's lots of fun.

She helps us all until our work is done.

Describe a teacher that you like.

Mr. Howard works hard so that we can succeed.

He helps us do math and he helps us read.

Describe a teacher that you like.

Mr. Chagolla, he lays down the law.

If you see him wrestle he'll leave you in awe.

Describe your principal.

Mrs. Dahlman makes our school a great place to be.

Our school is the best in the whole country.

HOOK

M – U – R – P – H – Y

We work hard so our dreams can fly.

LESSON

INTRODUCTION SONG

Objectives:
- Students will compose and perform a song introducing themselves – Standard(s) 1, 4

Lesson Length: Approx. 135 min. (three class periods)

Materials:
> Pencils
> Copies of Student Worksheets
> *Fresh Beats* CD

Procedure:
1. Read the following to students:
   "Earlier we wrote a song as a class. Today you are going to write a song introducing yourself."
2. Have students take out the "Introduction Song" worksheet.
3. Read the following to students:
   "On your worksheet there are several brackets. Each bracket has two lines and a topic written above. When you are writing your lyrics, choose a sentence that relates to the topic written above. Be sure that it can be spoken rhythmically and that it will fit into four beats. Once you have your first sentence, brainstorm words that rhyme with the final word of that sentence. For instance, if your first sentence is "we're here at school writing this song," you will want to find words that rhyme with "song" like "gong," "strong," or "wrong." Once you've decided on a rhyming word, write a sentence that ends with that word on the second line of the bracket."
4. Working on their own, give students three to five minutes to complete the first bracket of the "Introduction Song" worksheet in their workbooks. Play a background track from the *Fresh Beats* CD while students are working. Provide assistance as needed.
5. When students have completed the first bracket on their own, give them three to five minutes to share their work with others and collaborate as needed.
6. Repeat steps 4 and 5 for each bracket of verses 1, 2, and 3. When students have completed each verse, ask for volunteers to share their verse with the class. Students should *not* complete the "hook."
7. When students have completed all three verses, read the following:
   "Now that you have written your verses, the next step is to write your hook. Remember that the hook is the section of the song that summarizes its message. It's the part of the song that is easiest to remember. Your hook should be a summary of yourself."
8. Give students three to five minutes to complete their hook on their own. Play a background from the *Fresh Beats* CD while students are working. If students struggle with writing a first line, have them spell out their name.

   Example: "R – O – B – E – R – T"
         1   2 3   4
   "Doing my thing, so don't judge me."
      1   2   3   4

9. When students have completed their hooks, give them three to five minutes to share and collaborate with others.
10. Ask for volunteers to perform their song for the class.

Assessment:
Introduction Song Worksheet

INTRODUCTION SONG WORKSHEET

Use the following worksheet to complete your song. For every bracket, you will write two lines about the topic that is listed. Each pair of lines should end with rhyming words. Also, you should be able to recite each line and have it fit into four beats. Be sure to practice your lyrics out loud as you write them so that you know how they sound.

Introduce yourself. (2 points)

_____

_____

Describe yourself as a person. (2 points)

_____

_____

Tell where you are from. (2 points)

_____

_____

Describe where you live or who you live with. (2 points)

_____

_____

HOOK (2 points)

_____

_____

V
E
R
S
E

1

INTRODUCTION SONG WORKSHEET
(CONTINUED)

Tell where you go to school. (2 points)

_____

_____

Tell what grade you are in. (2 points)

**V
E
R
S
E**

_____

_____

Describe something that you like about your school. (2 points)

2

_____

_____

Describe what you do for fun. (2 points)

_____

_____

HOOK

_____

_____

Introduction Song Worksheet
(continued)

Describe something that is important to you. (2 points)

_____

_____

Describe what you want to be when you grow up. (2 points)

V
E   _____
R
S   _____
E

Describe what you will do to become what you want to be when you grow up. (2 points)

3   _____

_____

Give advice to others about living a good life. (2 points)

_____

_____

HOOK

_____

_____

Rubric for each pair of lines:

2 points	1 point	0 points
Both lines are complete and end with rhyming words	Both lines are complete but they do not end with rhyming words	At least one of the lines is incomplete

Grading: 26 – 24 points = A, 23 – 21 points = B, 20 – 19 points = C, 18 – 16 points = D, 15 – 0 points = F

INTRODUCTION SONG MODEL RESPONSE

Use the following worksheet to complete your class song. For every bracket, you will write two lines about the topic that is listed. Each pair of lines should end with rhyming words. Also, you should be able to recite each line and have it fit into four beats. Be sure to practice your lyrics out loud as you write them so that you know how they sound.

Introduce yourself. (2 points)

Hey everyone, it's me, Michelle.

My name sounds sweet like ringing a bell.

Describe yourself as a person. (2 points)

I do my best to have lots of fun.

But I can't go out until my work is done.

V E R S E

Tell where you are from. (2 points)

I was born and raised in Minneapolis.

Being there is like living in bliss.

1

Describe where you live or who you live with. (2 points)

I live at home with my family.

We've got a lot of people like branches on a tree.

HOOK (2 points)

M – I – C – H – E – L – L - E

I am who I am, don't try to change me.

INTRODUCTION SONG MODEL RESPONSE

Tell where you go to school. (2 points)

I go to school at Ira Murphy.

It's a great school, it's the place to be.

Tell what grade you are in. (2 points)

I'm in the ninth grade and I like it a lot.

I try to learn all the things that we get taught.

V E R S E 2

Describe something that you like about your school (2 points)

Math, yeah, it's my favorite class.

I get good grades so that I can pass.

Describe what you do for fun (2 points)

I like to dance because it's lots of fun.

I do it at night after school is done.

HOOK

M – I – C – H – E – L – L - E

I am who I am, don't try to change me.

INTRODUCTION SONG MODEL RESPONSE

Describe something that is important to you. (2 points)

V E R S E 3

My family is really important to me.

Without them I don't know where I'd be.

Describe what you want to be when you grow up. (2 points)

I want to be a teacher when I grow up.

Pouring out knowledge like I'm filling up a cup.

Describe what you will do to become what you want to be when you grow up (2 points)

Gotta get good grades so I can go to college.

Fill my brain with lots of knowledge.

Give advice to others about living a good life (2 points)

To live a good life you've got to be yourself.

You can't go around acting like somebody else.

HOOK

M – I – C – H – E – L – L - E

I am who I am, don't try to change me.

Rubric for each pair of lines:

2 points	1 point	0 points
Both lines are complete and end with rhyming words	Both lines are complete but they do not end with rhyming words	At least one of the lines is incomplete

Grading: 26 – 24 points = A, 23 – 21 points = B, 20 – 19 points = C, 18 – 16 points = D, 15 – 0 points = F

LESSON

SONG FOR CHANGE PREPARATION

Objectives:
- Students will summarize a news article
- Students will summarize something that they would like to change in the world

Lesson Length: Approx. 45 min. (one class period)

Materials:
Pencils
Copies of Student Worksheets
Newspaper

Procedure:
1. Read the following to students:
   "Over the next few days, you are going to write a song about something that you would like to change in the world. However, there are some things we need to do before we start. Today you are going to practice summarizing a story. This will be an important skill to have when you are writing your song. After that, we will prepare some information that you will use in your songs."
2. Have students take out the "Song for Change Preparation Story Summary" worksheet.
3. Break students into groups and give each group a newspaper clipping. Be sure that the clipping contains a complete story. Have students fill out the "Song for Change Preparation Story Summary" using their newspaper clipping.
4. Have students share their summaries with the class and provide clarification as needed.
5. Read the following to students:
   "Now that you've had practice summarizing stories, you're going to prepare to write a song about something that you want to change in the world."
6. Have students take out the "Song for Change Preparation Planning" worksheet.
7. In pairs, have students discuss something that they would like to change in the world.
8. Have students write their answers on the "topic" section of the "Song for Change Preparation Planning" worksheet. This will be the focus of their song.
9. After students have chosen a topic, have them fill out the rest of the "Song for Change Preparation Planning."
10. Have students share their summaries with a partner, and then with the class.

Assessment:
Song for Change Preparation Story Summary

SONG FOR CHANGE PREPARATION
STORY SUMMARY

Who was involved? (2 points)

_____

_____

What happened? (2 points)

_____

_____

_____

When did it happen? (2 points)

_____

Where did it happen? (2 points)

_____

Why did it happen? (2 points)

_____

_____

_____

Rubric for each question:

2 points	1 point	0 points
The response accurately answers the question	The response inaccurately answers the question	The question is not answered

Grading: 10 – 9 points = A, 8 points = B, 7 points = C, 6 points = D, 5 – 0 points = F

SONG FOR CHANGE PREPARATION
PLANNING

Topic:_____

What happens?

_____

_____

_____

_____

Why does it happen?

_____

_____

_____

_____

Who is involved and how?

_____

_____

_____

_____

When and where does it happen?

_____

_____

SONG FOR CHANGE PREPARATION
PLANNING (CONTINUED)

Why should it change?

_____

_____

_____

_____

What will need to happen for it to change?

_____

_____

_____

_____

What can people do right now to change it?

_____

_____

_____

_____

_____

LESSON

SONG FOR CHANGE

Objectives:
- Students will compose and perform a song about something that they would like to change in the world – Standard(s) 1, 4

Duration: Approx. 90 min. (two class periods)

Materials:
>Pencils
>Copies of Student Worksheets
>*Fresh Beats* CD

Procedure:
1. Read the following to students:
"Yesterday you described something that you would like to change in the world. This is going to be the topic of the song that you are going to begin today. The first section of your song will describe the thing that you'd like to change. The second will convince people that it should change and give them solutions."
2. Have students turn to the "Song for Change" worksheet in their workbooks.
3. Read the following to students:
"In your workbook are several brackets. Each bracket has two lines and a topic written above. When you are writing your lyrics, choose a sentence that relates to the topic written above. Once you have your first sentence, brainstorm words that rhyme with the final word of that sentence. For instance, if your first sentence is "we're here at school writing this song," you will want to find words that rhyme with "song" like "gong," "strong," or "wrong." Once you've decided on a rhyming word, write a sentence that ends with that word on the second line of the bracket. Use the "Song for Change Preparation Planning" worksheet as a guide."
4. Working on their own, give students three to five minutes to complete the first bracket of the "Song for Change" worksheet in their workbooks. Play a background track from the *Fresh Beats* CD while students are working. Provide assistance as needed.
5. When students have completed the first bracket on their own, give them three to five minutes to share their work with others and collaborate as needed.
6. Repeat steps 4 and 5 for each bracket of verses 1 and 2. When students have completed each verse, ask for volunteers to share with the class. Students should *not* complete the "hook."
7. When students have completed both verses, read the following:
"Now that you have written your verses, the next step is to write your hook. Remember that the hook is the section of the song that summarizes its message. It's the part of the song that is easiest to remember because it repeats throughout the song. Your hook should summarize the message of your song."
8. Give students three to five minutes to complete their hook on their own. Play a background from the *Fresh Beats* CD while students are working.
9. When students have completed their hooks, give them three to five minutes to share and collaborate with others.
10. Ask for volunteers to perform their song for the class.

Assessment:
Song for Change Worksheet

Song for Change Worksheet

Use the following worksheet to complete your song. For every bracket, you will write two lines about the topic that is listed. Each pair of lines should end with rhyming words. Also, you should be able to recite each line and have it fit into four beats. Be sure to practice your lyrics out loud as you write them so that you know how they sound.

What you would like to change? (2 points)

_____

_____

Who is involved? (2 points)

_____

_____

V
E *Where does it happen? (2 points)*
R
S _____
E
       _____
1

When does it happen? (2 points)

_____

_____

Why does it happen? (2 points)

_____

_____

HOOK (2 points)

_____

_____

SONG FOR CHANGE WORKSHEET
(CONTINUED)

Why is this important to you? (2 points)

_____

_____

V
E
R
S
E

2

Why should it change? (2 points)

_____

_____

What can people do to change it? (2 points)

_____

_____

What would the world be like if it changed? (2 points)

_____

_____

HOOK

_____

_____

Rubric for each pair of lines:

2 points	1 point	0 points
Both lines are complete and end with rhyming words	Both lines are complete but they do not end with rhyming words	At least one of the lines is incomplete

Grading: 20 – 18 points = A, 17 – 16 points = B, 15 – 14 points = C, 13 – 12 points = D, 11 – 0 points = F

SONG FOR CHANGE MODEL RESPONSE

Use the following worksheet to complete your song. For every bracket, you will write two lines about the topic that is listed. Each pair of lines should end with rhyming words. Also, you should be able to recite each line and have it fit into four beats. Be sure to practice your lyrics out loud as you write them so that you know how they sound.

What you would like to change? (2 points)

Drug abuse is something that I hate.

I hope that people stop before it's too late.

Who is involved? (2 points)

People use drugs at all ages.

If their life were a book they'd be losing pages.

VERSE 1

Where does it happen? (2 points)

Drug abuse happens all over the world.

It affects every man, woman, boy, and girl.

When does it happen? (2 points)

It's been going on since the dawn of time.

If you see what drugs do you'll know why using is a crime.

Why does it happen? (2 points)

People use drugs when they're upset or stressed.

Sometimes they'll use them so they won't feel depressed.

HOOK (2 points)

Drugs are messing up the world so let's take a stand.

Make a better place for every woman and man.

Song for Change Model Response
(continued)

Why is this important to you.? (2 points)

<u>I know people who do drugs and it messes up their heads.</u>

<u>I care about them and don't want to see them dead.</u>

Why should it change? (2 points)

<u>Drugs make the world a darker place.</u>

<u>Some people say I'm wrong but I know that's not the case.</u>

What can people do to change it? (2 points)

<u>We can stop drug abuse by helping others out.</u>

<u>Show them there are other ways to work their problems out.</u>

What would the world be like if it changed? (2 points)

<u>Without drugs people would live better lives.</u>

<u>They'd be better sons, daughters, husbands, and wives.</u>

V E R S E 2

HOOK

<u>Drugs are messing up the world so let's take a stand.</u>

<u>Make a better world for every woman and man.</u>

Rubric for each pair of lines:

2 points	1 point	0 points
Both lines are complete and end with rhyming words	Both lines are complete but they do not end with rhyming words	At least one of the lines is incomplete

Grading: 20 – 18 points = A, 17 – 16 points = B, 15 – 14 points = C, 13 – 12 points = D, 11 – 0 points = F

RECORDING

After students have written their songs, you may want to record them. There are several options for this. The most basic method of recording requires a digital voice recorder. Should you choose this method, have students recite their lyrics while a background track from the *Fresh Beats* CD plays. Use the digital voice recorder to record students' performances.

Those with more technological resources may choose to use one of a number of computer recording programs such as GarageBand or Pro Tools. Those using computer programs will need several things: a microphone that connects to their computer, two pairs of headphones, and a splitter for the headphone jacks. To record students, connect the microphone and headphones to the computer. Use the splitter to allow two people to listen to the computer's audio. Be sure that the program you are using recognizes the microphone as the source of audio input.

Most programs use tracks to record and store individual parts or instruments. Be sure that you have created a track specifically for your recording and that it is receiving information from your microphone.

When recording, the person who is being recorded and the person operating the computer should each wear a set of headphones. This allows both people to hear audio from the computer without it being picked up by the microphone.

Students may have difficulty getting through their entire piece in one "take," so it helps to break songs up into smaller sections when recording. Consider creating multiple tracks, recording different sections of the song on each track, and then splicing them together.

Most programs allow you to create multiple background tracks. The following suggestions may help guide you and your students as they create interesting backgrounds for their songs:

- Begin by creating an introduction using either a drum beat or an instrumental track.

- Bring in the first verse after the introduction and add a new instrument to the background. If you used a drum beat as your introduction, bring in an instrumental track or if you used an instrumental track, bring in a drumbeat.

- For each verse, keep at least one instrumental track the same as the previous verse while adding or subtracting others to keep the song interesting.

- Try to make the hook stand out from the verses by keeping at least one track the same while changing another.

- Consider putting a break between verses and hooks if the transitions are awkward.

- Experiment with how the backgrounds can reflect the mood or overall affect of the song. If the mood of the song changes, how could the backgrounds reflect that?

- If your school has an instrumental music program, consider using musicians from those classes to help create backgrounds.

* These are only a few options for how to structure a song. They are intended solely as suggestions. Teachers and students are encouraged to explore multiple possibilities for formal structures.

DRUM SET

LESSON

DRUM SET — BASIC ROCK/HIP-HOP BEAT

Objectives:
- Students will read and perform a basic rock/hip-hop beat – Standard(s) 2, 5

Duration: Approx. 45 min. (one class period)

Materials:
Drum Set Worksheet
Recordings of the following:
- "Killing Me Softly" by Lauryn Hill and the Fugees
- "Gettin' Jiggy With It" by Will Smith (optional)
Drum set (optional)

*These two songs both use the drum set pattern learned in this lesson. **However, "Gettin' Jiggy With It" contains language that may be inappropriate for some classrooms.** "Killing Me Softly" is a "clean" alternative but does not contain rapping, though many elements are taken from hip-hop.*

Procedures:
1. Read the following to students:
   "Early DJs and MCs did not have beat machines or computers to help them create their music. Instead, they used funk and rock records. As a result, hip-hop beats evolved out of funk and rock beats. Today you are going to learn to play a basic rock/hip-hop beat."
2. Have students turn take out the "Basic Rock/Hip-Hop Beat Worksheet."
3. As a class, count rhythms 1, 2, and 3 in the student workbook individually. You may choose to use the *Fresh Beats* CD as it has recordings of each rhythm being read and performed.
4. Using their *right* hand, have students play and count rhythm #1 on their *left* knee.
5. It is very important when playing drum set that students be able to play multiple rhythms without paying special attention any single rhythm. In order to facilitate this, have students count and play rhythm # 1 while you ask them to do a series of tasks with their left hand like "point to the ceiling, touch your year, point to someone wearing green, etc."
6. Once students are comfortable playing rhythm #1 have them place their *left* hand on their *left* thigh. Using their *left* hand, have students play and count rhythm #2 on their *left* thigh.
7. Using their *right* foot, have students play and count rhythm #3.
8. Using their *right* foot and *left* hand, have students play rhythms #2 and #3 together while counting "one, two, three, four." They should alternate between playing with their foot and their hand.
9. Have students continue to play rhythms #2 and #3, but ask them to count rhythm #1 (eighth-notes) as they play.
10. When students are comfortable counting rhythm #1 and playing rhythms #2 and #3, have them add rhythm #1 with their *right* hand on their *left* knee.
11. Play "Killing Me Softly" while students practice the drum set pattern.

    If students have trouble playing all three parts simultaneously, have them isolate two until they are comfortable enough to add the third.

12. If a drum set is available, allow volunteers to play while the class practices using their bodies. When students play the drum set, rhythm #1 is played on a closed high-hat, rhythm #2 is played on the snare drum, and rhythm #3 is played on the bass drum.

Assessment:
Basic Rock/Hip-Hop Beat Playing Test

Basic Rock/Hip-Hop Beat Worksheet

Early DJs and MCs did not have beat machines or computers to help them create their music. Instead, they used funk and rock records. As a result, hip-hop beats evolved out of funk and rock beats. The rhythms below, when played together, create a basic rock/hip-hop beat.

Count the rhythms below individually. You can refer to your *Fresh Beats* CD to hear how each rhythm is counted and played.

Rhythm #1

Rhythm #2

Rhythm #3

Using your *right* hand, play rhythm #1 on your *left* knee. Be sure to say the counts out loud.

Rhythm #1

Once you are comfortable playing rhythm #1, it's time to move on to rhythm #2.
Using your *left* hand, play rhythm #2 on your *left* thigh. Be sure to say the counts out loud.

Rhythm #2

Using your *right* foot, play rhythm #3. Be sure to say the counts out loud.

Rhythm #3

Once you are comfortable performing each rhythm individually, play rhythm #2 and rhythm #3 simultaneously. You should say "1, 2, 3, 4" continuously while playing, and alternate between your right foot and your left hand as you count.

Example:
Body Part Being Used: Foot – Hand – Foot – Hand – Foot – Hand – Foot – Hand
Number Being Counted: 1   2   3   4   1   2   3   4

Rhythm #2

(1)   2   (3)   4   (1)   2   (3)   4

Rhythm #3

1   (2)   3   (4)   1   (2)   3   (4)

Once you are comfortable performing rhythm #2 and rhythm #3, play rhythm #1, rhythm #2, and rhythm #3 simultaneously while counting rhythm #1 out loud.

Rhythm #1

1 & 2 & 3 & 4 &   1 & 2 & 3 & 4 &

Rhythm #2

(1)   2   (3)   4   (1)   2   (3)   4

Rhythm #3

1   (2)   3   (4)   1   (2)   3   (4)

Once you are comfortable performing these rhythms on your body, you are ready to perform using a drum set. Rhythm #1 is played by the right hand on a closed high-hat. Rhythm #2 is played by the left hand on the snare drum. Rhythm #3 is played by the right foot on the bass drum.

PLAYING TEST

BASIC ROCK/HIP-HOP BEAT

Student Name: _____

Playing Parts Individually

3 Points	2 Points	1 Point	0 Points
Student can play all individual parts accurately	Student can play two individual parts accurately	Student can play one part accurately	Student cannot play any part accurately

Playing Parts Simultaneously

3 Points	2 Points	1 Point	0 Points
Student can play all parts accurately simultaneously	Student can play two parts accurately simultaneously	Student can play one part accurately	Student cannot play any part accurately

Continuity

2 Points	1 Point	0 Points
Student plays without stopping	Student plays with occasional stops	Student plays with frequent stops

Tempo

2 Points	1 Point	0 Points
Student plays with a consistent tempo	Student plays with minor tempo changes	Student plays with severe tempo fluctuations

Total Score:_____

Grading:
10 – 9 points = A, 8 points = B, 7 points = C, 6 points = D, 5 – 0 points = F

LESSON

BEAT #2

Objectives:
- Students will read and perform a hip-hop beat – Standard(s) 2, 5
- Students will compare and contrast drum patterns in two songs – Standard(s) 6

Duration: Approx. 45 min. (one class period)

Materials:
Copies of Beat #2 Worksheet
Recordings of the Following:
- "U Can't Touch This" by MC Hammer
- "Killing Me Softly" by Lauryn Hill and The Fugees
- "Gettin' Jiggy Wit' It" by Will Smith (optional)
Drum Set (optional)

Both "Killing Me Softly" and "Gettin' Jiggy Wit' It" use the basic beat learned in the previous lesson.
However, "Gettin' Jiggy With It" contains language that may be inappropriate for some classrooms. "Killing Me Softly" is a "clean" alternative but does not contain rapping though it is still has hip-hop elements and was recorded by a hip-hop group.

Procedures:
1. Begin by reviewing the basic rock beat learned in the previous lesson.

2. Have students practice the basic rock beat while listening to "Killing Me Softly" by Lauryn Hill and The Fugees.

3. Play "U Can't Touch This" by MC Hammer. Ask students to listen for differences between the drum parts for "U Can't Touch This" and "Killing Me Softly."

4. Have students share their answers with a partner, and then with the class.

5. Explain to students that "U Can't Touch This" and "Killing Me Softly" use the same basic drum pattern with the exception of the bass drum.

6. Play "U Can't Touch This" and ask students to clap the bass drum rhythm with the song.

7. Read the following to students:
   "Earlier you learned how to play a basic rock beat. Today you are going to learn a variation of that beat that is often used in hip-hop and is similar to the one used in U Can't Touch This."

8. Have students take out the "Hip-Hop Beat Worksheet."

9. As a class, count rhythms #1, #2, and #3. You may choose to use the *Fresh Beats* CD as it has recordings of each rhythm being read and performed.

10. Using their *right* hand, have students play and count rhythm #1 on their *left* knee.

11. It is very important when playing drum set that students be able to play multiple rhythms without paying special attention to them. In order to facilitate this, have students count and play rhythm # 1 while you ask them to do a series of tasks with their left hand like "point to the ceiling, touch your year, point to someone wearing green, etc."

12. Once students are comfortable playing rhythm #1, have them place their *left* hand on their *left* thigh. Using the *left* hand, have students play and count rhythm #2 on their *left* thigh.

13. Using their *right* foot, have students play and count rhythm #3.

14. Using their *right* foot and *left* hand, have students play rhythms #2 and #3 together while counting "one – two - & - three – four &." This is the composite of rhythms #2 and #3:

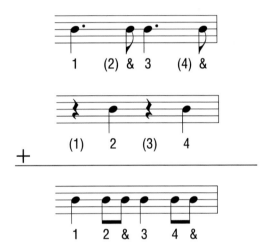

15. Have students continue to play rhythms #2 and #3 but ask them to count rhythm #1 (eighth notes) as they play.

16. When students are comfortable counting rhythm #1 and playing rhythms #2 and #3, have them add rhythm #1 with their *right* hand on their *left* knee.

17. Play "U Can't Touch This" while students practice the drum set pattern.

    If students have trouble playing all three parts simultaneously, have them isolate two until they are comfortable enough to add the third.

18. If a drum set is available, allow volunteers to play while the class practices using their bodies. When students play the drum set, rhythm #1 is played on a closed high-hat, rhythm #2 is played on the snare drum, and rhythm #3 is played on the bass drum.

Assessment:
Hip-Hop Beat Playing Test

BEAT #2 WORKSHEET

The rhythms below, when played together, form a beat that is used in many genres, including hip-hop. You will notice that rhythm #1 and rhythm #2 are the same as the basic rock/hip-hop beat. The only thing that has changed is rhythm # 3 (the bass drum part). You may use your *Fresh Beats* CD as a guide while practicing.

Rhythm #1

Rhythm #2

Rhythm #3

Using your *right* hand, play rhythm #1 on your *left* knee. Be sure to say the counts out loud.

Rhythm #1

Once you are comfortable playing rhythm #1, it's time to move on to rhythm #2.
Using your *left* hand, play rhythm #2 on your *left* thigh. Be sure to say the counts out loud.

Rhythm #2

Using your *right* foot, play rhythm #3. Be sure to say the counts out loud.

Rhythm #3

Once you are comfortable performing each rhythm individually, play rhythm #2 and rhythm #3 simultaneously. You should say "1 - 2 & - 3 - 4 &" because it is the combination of the two rhythms. "1" should be played by your *right* foot. "2" should be played by your *left* hand. "& 3" should be played by your *right* foot. "4" should be played by your *left* hand.

Rhythm #2

Rhythm #3

Once you are comfortable performing rhythm #2 and rhythm #3, play rhythm #1, rhythm #2, and rhythm #3 simultaneously while counting rhythm #1 out loud.

Rhythm #1

Rhythm #2

Rhythm #3

Once you are comfortable performing these rhythms on your body, you are ready to perform using a drum set. Rhythm #1 is played by the right hand on a closed high-hat. Rhythm #2 is played by the left hand on the snare drum. Rhythm #3 is played by the right foot on the bass drum.

DRUM BEAT #2 PLAYING TEST

Student Name: _____

Playing Parts Individually

3 Points	2 Points	1 Point	0 Points
Student can play all individual parts accurately	Student can play two individual parts accurately	Student can play one part accurately	Student cannot play any part accurately

Playing Parts Simultaneously

3 Points	2 Points	1 Point	0 Points
Student can play all parts accurately simultaneously	Student can play two parts accurately simultaneously	Student can play one part accurately	Student cannot play any parts accurately

Continuity

2 Points	1 Point	0 Points
Student plays without stopping	Student plays with occasional stops	Student plays with frequent stops

Tempo

2 Points	1 Point	0 Points
Student plays with a consistent tempo	Student plays with minor tempo changes	Student plays with severe tempo fluctuations

Total Score: _____

Grading:
10 – 9 points = A, 8 points = B, 7 points = C, 6 points = D, 5 – 0 points = F

LESSON

DRUM SET COMPOSITION

Objectives:
- Students will compose and perform a drum set pattern – Standard(s) 2, 4

Duration: Approx. 45 min. (1 class period)

Materials:
Whiteboard/Marker
Drum Set (optional)

Procedures:

1. Write the following on the board:

Rhythm #1

Rhythm #2

2. Read the following to students:

   "So far you have learned to play two different drum beats. Today you will work in groups to compose and perform your own beat."

3. Divide students into groups of three.

4. Using their *right* hand, have students count and play rhythm 1 on their *left* knee.

5. Using their *left* hand, have students count and play rhythm 2 on their *left* thigh.

6. Read the following to students:

   "Now that we've reviewed the rhythms for the high-hat and snare drum, as a group I would like for you to create a new bass drum rhythm. The rhythm must fit within four beats. It also must be able to be played by your right foot."

7. Give students three to five minutes to compose a bass drum rhythm as a group. These rhythms do not need to be written down.

    If students struggle with composing a rhythm, have them choose a word or series of words and say them rhythmically.

    Examples:

8. Using their *right* foot, have each group perform their bass drum rhythm for the class.

9. Give students three to five minutes to practice performing rhythm 2 and their composed rhythm simultaneously. Students should use their *left* hand to perform rhythm 2 and their *right* foot to perform their composed rhythm. Provide assistance as needed.

10. When students are comfortable performing rhythm 2 and their composed rhythm simultaneously, give them three to five minutes to practice performing rhythm 1, rhythm 2, and their composed rhythm simultaneously.

    If students have trouble playing all three parts simultaneously, have them isolate two until they are comfortable enough to add the third.

19. If a drum set is available, allow volunteers to play while the class practices using their bodies. When students play the drum set, rhythm 1 is played on a closed high-hat, rhythm two is played on the snare drum, and rhythm three is played on the bass drum.

Assessment:
Drum Set Composition Playing Test

PLAYING TEST

DRUM SET COMPOSITION

Student Name: _____

Playing Parts Individually

3 Points	2 Points	1 Point	0 Points
Student can play all individual parts accurately	Student can play two individual parts accurately	Student can play one part accurately	Student cannot play any part accurately

Playing Parts Simultaneously

3 Points	2 Points	1 Point	0 Points
Student can play all parts accurately simultaneously	Student can play two parts accurately simultaneously	Student can play one part accurately	Student cannot play any parts accurately

Continuity

2 Points	1 Point	0 Points
Student plays without stopping	Student plays with occasional stops	Student plays with frequent stops

Tempo

2 Points	1 Point	0 Points
Student plays with a consistent tempo	Student plays with minor tempo changes	Student plays with severe tempo fluctuations

Total Score:_____

Grading:
10 – 9 points = A, 8 points = B, 7 points = C, 6 points = D, 5 – 0 points = F

NOTES

Notes